DOWN THE BOOKIES

DOWN THE BOOKIES

THE FIRST 50 YEARS OF BETTING SHOPS

JOHN SAMUELS

RACING POST

DEDICATION

This book is dedicated to my wonderful wife Linda, our children
Lisa and Jon-Paul, grandchildren Charlotte, Alex, Millie and Luke.
Not forgetting my son-in-law, Robert, and daughter-in-law, Hannah.

This edition first published in Great Britain in 2011 by
Racing Post Books
Axis House, Compton, Newbury, Berkshire, RG20 6NL

1 3 5 7 9 10 8 6 4 2

ISBN 978-1-908216-17-5

Designed by Fiona Pike

Printed and bound in Great Britain by the MPG Books Group

www.racingpost.com/shop

CONTENTS

ACKNOWLEDGEMENTS

Where to start in thanking people for their help and support in the writing of this book?

Certainly it would not have seen the light of day were it not for my wife Linda.

Likewise David Ashforth and Jim Cremin, both of the *Racing Post*, who volunteered to read the early drafts and encouraged me to plough on when I wanted to give up.

Many thanks also to the team at *Racing Post* publications, James de Wesselow and Julian Brown, and to John Cobb for their editing.

Others who read early drafts, helped me with recollections and made suggestions for improvement include Paul Bellringer OBE, Chris Bird, Peter Brewin, Chris Cyronni (Ladbrokes security director), Andrew Fraser, Andrew McCarron (Editor of *Betting Business Interactive*), Louise Newman (Betview), Chris Pitt (BOS), Lesley Sharman (Chief executive of BOS) and George White.

I would also like to thank Andrew Lyman (head of public affairs at William Hill) and Stu McInroy (Bookmakers Committee at the Horserace Betting Levy Board) for their assistance in researching Betting Levy facts.

Finally, I must thank everyone alluded to, but not mentioned by name. And, most importantly, a big thank you to those colleagues and friends I have met along the way and who have helped my career, and thus indirectly helped create this book.

FOREWORD

Sometimes I return to the High Street in Wealdstone where I spent my formative years, but I don't really enjoy going back.

Back then, I loved visiting Carne's record shop with my mate John Maule where we'd each buy one of that week's hit singles for 6/8d. I have collected records ever since.

There was a second-hand bookshop where I'd snap up a bargain volume – if I couldn't find what I wanted I'd borrow it from the library. I have a huge collection of books now.

My mum would send me on errands – to buy stuff from Woolworths, grocery shop Victor Value, Mac Fisheries, Spurriers the baker's, Dewhurst the butcher's.

You can probably see where I'm going with this: record shops, second-hand books, all those branded shops – even libraries – are all endangered species or already extinct.

But also nestling in that high street was a betting shop, which I visited on a regular basis. Not, admittedly, when they opened legally in 1961 – I was just ten at the time – but not long after I'd found ways and means of becoming a regular customer.

Another mate Graham Brown and I would meet every Saturday to pick horses in each race of the day, using a complicated scoring scheme to determine who was the better tipster. To our delight, Graham's dad sometimes took us racing to Goodwood, where we'd stand on Trundle Hill and absorb the atmosphere.

In that betting shop in Wealdstone I devised the surefire system of backing the prolific hunter chaser Baulking Green and the dashing Hackney-based greyhound Ba The Rover every time they ran. The excitement of picking out a horse and then backing it would never fade, and we both became lifelong punters – I've now been racing on five different continents and not once lost the urge to have a flutter.

Once I was old enough to inhabit betting shops on a legal footing I fell completely in love with their slightly seedy but irresistible mixture of dodgy blokes, welcoming banter and the thrilling, adrenaline-pumping prospect of departing with more money than I had when I went in.

My farewell gift from my job as journalist on a newspaper was money to spend in the betting shop. Newly unemployed, I spent a few weeks in the betting shop with fellow dole recipient and incurable punting optimist Chuff Trainer, before deciding I wanted to work in a betting shop full time – and I've been in the business ever since.

From the moment they were made legal, betting shops were put on the back foot, by a 'delicate hypocrisy' typical of the British. The public was allowed betting shops, but they weren't allowed to be attractive or welcoming, with television screens or refreshments.

But bookies have never understood the concept of defeat and although the betting shop laws were unchanged until 1986, they still catered imaginatively for their clientele. Once the shackles were eased and such luxuries as cups of tea were permitted, they became an essential, established and vibrant feature of Britain's high streets.

Today, 99 per cent of betting shops are still there, solid and dependable, while so many other businesses have faded away. Self-interest groups and vote-seeking politicians often rage unintelligibly against betting shops replacing yet another failed business. Would they prefer more empty shops?

I've had wonderful times in betting shops as a nervous rookie punter, a boardman, settler, manager and regular gambler. And to judge by his vivid recollections, affectionate anecdotes and insightful look back at the history of half a century of betting shops – so has John Samuels.

As you follow him through the pages and the years you'll meet an amazing cast of colourful characters and enjoy John's entertaining punting-based experiences and adventures.

Anyone who has spent even the shortest amount of time in one of these unique, misunderstood establishments will recognise in John's terrific book their real strengths and their few weaknesses.

As the high street struggles to survive, you can bet that the betting shop will be among the last to close its doors and disappear into virtual cyberspace where so much of life is now being conducted. It would not be the same without it.

Graham Sharpe
Media Relations Director
William Hill

GROWING UP

A Cockney Upbringing, Working for Ladbrokes,
The Three-Card Trick, Betting Shops in the 1830s,
Football Pools, Illegal Street Betting, Prince Monolulu,
Greyhound Racing, Tic Tac and Signals

May 2011, I am 63 years of age, betting shops have been in existence for exactly 50 years and I have been in the industry my whole life.

I was born in Mile End Hospital in Stepney, London, to an impoverished couple who had just suffered the agonies of the Second World War. The early months of 1947 presented the worst winter in living memory and many resorted to time-honoured ways of keeping warm. One consequence was my conception and thus, nine months later, John Samuels – it has often been said my parents could not afford a middle name – entered life.

I was the second of what were to be four sons and, being born within the sound of Bow bells, I was a true cockney.

There is much confusion about what constitutes a cockney. To those from outside London, a cockney is anyone born in the capital. For some Londoners anyone born between the area east of Holborn and the suburbs of Essex is a cockney. Some East Londoners believe a cockney is anyone born within the sound of the bells at Bow church – that stands in an island in the middle of the road that runs from Bow to Stratford.

But, as others may know, the Bow church referred to for the cockney label 'Born within the sound of Bow bells', is St Mary-le-Bow, at Cheapside, in the City of London. And the sound of these bells can only be heard across the river in Southwark, west to Fleet Street, north to parts of Islington and east to Stepney Green.

Both my parents were of lower working-class stock. My dad had his roots in the East End of London and his grandparents were Jewish immigrants from Eastern Europe. Mum came from a coal-mining family from the northeast of England. Her ancestry was Roman Catholic and her Irish grandparents had emigrated to Britain due to the potato famine in Ireland. Not a good start for me and the other sons in the family, and certainly no silver spoons or family inheritance in sight.

Home was a prefab in Limehouse, the heart of the East End. Prefabs were hastily built housing units, placed on what were once bomb sites. They were supposed to be temporary until more permanent, conventional housing was built for the homecoming heroes from the war. Our family lived in one for 15 'temporary' years.

At the end of primary school I somehow managed to get a place at one of the few Catholic grammar schools in London, where I enjoyed maths and English.

In my formative childhood years I would roam the streets, playing games with friends until dark, make occasional shoplifting trips to the likes of Woolworth's and annoy the neighbourhood with pranks such as knock down ginger.

I saw some serious fights between adults over street card game disputes, or a two bob up the wall – otherwise known as pitch and toss. Pitch and toss is a street gambling game, played for any stakes. Any coin can be used but every player must use the same. Each person, in turn, tosses their coin against a wall about five metres away. The one whose coin finishes nearest to the wall wins all the stakes. In its own way it is quite a skilful game but arguments often ensued when two coins appeared to be the same distance from the wall. Being an illegal gaming activity the players could not call a police officer to adjudicate.

Keeping look-out for the illegal street bookies, getting into scrapes, playing football in the streets was all part of the mix – as well as enforced attendance at Sunday Mass and alter serving. All quite normal for a young Catholic lad being brought up in the East End.

Penny for the guying, selling chopped up apple and orange boxes for firewood, and other forms of entrepreneurship put me in good stead for later life and taught me how to deal with the public.

At 16, I wanted to get out into the real world and chose not to go into higher education – a decision I have rarely regretted. So I left school for a job in the credit-control department of Ladbrokes in their office at Ganton Street, Soho, in the heart of London.

What an eye-opener. The office was just off Carnaby Street and the Swinging Sixties was just kicking off. There were all kinds of music clubs within walking distance, including The Marquee, Whiskey-A-Go-Go and The Flamingo, where such Sixties icons as The Kinks, The Animals, Manfred Mann, The Moody Blues and Yardbirds performed.

At 16, I felt I was right in the heart of things, but I had a lot to learn. Working in London's West End, it was common to see the confidence tricks that were (and still are) played on the streets. I ask myself how I fell for one – the Find the Lady street-card game.

Feeling flush with my week's salary in my pocket, I was walking down Wardour Street when I came across a crowd gathered round a man huddled over an upturned wooden crate.

For younger readers it should be explained that, until the 1980s, wages were often paid weekly in cash. And wooden crates were everywhere, outside greengrocers, fruit and vegetable shops, all waiting to be collected by the refuse van.

The crates were used as a table, on which the dealer would place three cards. As he did so, he showed them to the crowds: the two of clubs, two of hearts and queen of diamonds. He turned the cards face down on the table and offer to pay 2-1 to anyone who could say which card was the lady (queen of diamonds) – but there were no takers.

He tried again. Each time he placed the two of clubs between his thumb and forefinger in one hand; the queen of diamonds and two of hearts between the thumb and forefinger of his other hand and, with a flick of his wrist, all the cards would end up face down on the table. 'Find the lady, 2-1,' he shouted. I didn't think the odds were bad, but there were still no takers.

Suddenly, someone dropped a £5 note on the floor, distracting the card dealer and the crowd as they turned to look at the commotion. A man standing nearby took his chance to steal a quick peek at the cards. He then indicated to the crowd where the queen (lady) was – in line with where most spectators thought she was anyway. This time, when the man shouted: '2-1 find the lady,' he was almost knocked over in the rush to place bets. With the money (my own included) on the table the cards were turned over and the lady was not where it should have been. 'That's all for today folks,' said the card dealer, and in a flash he was gone, with all our money.

The crowd were dumbstruck. Then it slowly dawned. The card dealer had not been distracted; the man who looked at the cards had intentionally misled the crowd. And the dropped £5 note? It was all part of the con. The card dealer had used quickness of the hand to deceive the eye in putting the queen in a place where no one would suspect it was.

No wonder the odds being offered of 2-1, on a three-possibility event, were good. The card dealer and his gang were betting on a certainty. Within seconds of the cards being turned over, and before the crowd had realised what had happened, all three of the gang were off and out of sight. I had been turned over by, what I later learnt, was the oldest con in the book, the three-card trick. 'What a plonker, not so clever now,' I thought to myself. How could I explain to my parents that I had no money and could not make my normal contribution to the housekeeping bills that week?

Even now I break into a cold sweat when I think about that embarrassing day. I had heard talk of the three-card trick but didn't know what it was. Why hadn't my dad told me about this, he must have known? Maybe it was intentional, and dad wanted me to learn the hard way.

I was never caught again, in any way, always remembering the old adages: 'if something is too good to be true, it almost certainly is' and 'you can only con the foolish, the dishonest, and the greedy'.

Why did I go into the bookmaking industry? Maybe it had something to do with my speed with arithmetic; but maybe more so that my dad was a lifelong inveterate gambler.

My Dad, Fred, was more often than not out of paid work, and for as far back as I can remember he lost his weekly dole and sickness benefit payments to the local bookies. The dole payment was a small sum given by the government to anyone who was unemployed; sickness benefit was paid to Fred as he had been discharged from the Royal Air Force with ill health after the Second World War.

I considered working for Ladbrokes was a way of getting some of dad's losses back. More importantly, I wanted to be on the other side of the counter, taking the punters' money, rather than losing it from the punters' side.

When I started my working life, betting shops had only been legal again for a few years, after being outlawed in 1853.

During the early 1800s betting offices were called list houses because lists of the days runners would be pinned to their walls. They were everywhere – an estimated 400 in London alone – and used by both men and women.

But there was a growing anti-gambling lobby whose members believed that if the aristocracy wanted to bet, and lose money, that was their choice as they could afford it. They believed temptation should be removed from the lower classes of society.

Consider the painting *The Derby Day*, by William Powell Frith in 1858, which can be seen in London's Tate Gallery. It is a picture that captures a moment in time on Epsom Downs on Derby Day. There is colour, romance, greed, excitement, entertainment and a host of other emotions depicted.

See the ragamuffins in the foreground whose parents, if they have any, probably squandered what little they had on betting or gin. See also to the left, the woman who is trying to dissuade her husband from getting involved in the gambling that is taking place on the table next to him. They are both, no doubt, fresh from a farm in the country and he already has his hand in his pocket and is itching to have a bet. Something tells me she is worldlier then he, or maybe she can see the gentleman with the top hat, who is looking bemused because, in all probability, he has just lost all he had at the betting game, probably Crown and Anchor or possibly Find the Lady or similar, taking place at the table. Or maybe he has just been the subject of an attack by a pickpocket. No doubt the man in the red coat, with his waving arm in the air, is trying to convince those who will listen that he knows the winner of the Derby and for a few pence will share his knowledge.

If nothing else, this 1858 painting reminds us that gambling is not new and indeed has been with us for centuries. But maybe there is a hidden message too, as a warning for the poor working class. The anti-gambling lobby believed that, for those at the bottom of the social scale, betting led to debt, which led to crime. And betting, together with the notion of getting something for nothing, weakened the fabric of family life.

The anti-gambling lobby was strong and influential. The Attorney General noted: 'the mischief arising from the existence of the betting shops was perfectly notorious'. It was also the case that many owners of these list houses would abscond should they experience a series of bad results.

Charles Dickens wrote in 1852: 'Betting shops spring up in every street! There is a demand at all the brokers' shops for old fly-blown, coloured prints of racehorses, and for any odd folio volumes that have the appearance of Ledgers. Two such prints in any shop window and one such book on a shop counter, will make a complete Betting Office'. Not exactly a glowing testament to the professionalism of the industry of the time.

But not many of the betting shops had good financial backing. More often than not, crowds could be seen gathering outside, trying to collect their winnings, only to realise that the owner had 'done a runner'. The cartoon by John Leech, circa 1850, entitled *Bolted* probably sums it up.

"BOLTED!"

So, after pressure from many influential quarters, the government of the day introduced the 1853 Betting Houses Act which prevented premises, apart from private clubs such as Tattersalls, to be used for the placing of a bet.

The Act might have closed the list houses, but betting activity simply moved, in the main, to public houses. Consequently the 1872 Licensing Act was passed, giving penalties to persons who allowed their licensed premises to be used for betting.

Ever an entrepreneurial body, the bookmakers again continued their trade – this time on the streets. Typically the bookmaker would stand in an area where a group could gather without causing too much of an obstruction under a large umbrella – hence on-course bookmakers today are typically to be seen standing beneath large umbrellas.

Subsequently, in an effort to stamp out these practices, the Street Betting Act of 1906 was passed. Again this had little success as it merely heightened the excitement of betting and illegal bookmakers thrived. The police also found the Act difficult to enforce, as is always the case with unpopular laws.

For those who did not want to step across the legal boundary and use street bookmakers there were also local raffles, newspaper 'spot the ball' competitions, and the once very popular football pools coupon bets.

Newspapers ran spot the ball competitions. They printed an action picture from the football pitch – minus the ball – which the punters are required to predict the centre of in the picture.

As is frequently the case with gamblers, many spot the ball players thought the whole thing was a conspiracy. Stories told how apparently accurate predictions were judged to be incorrect so that relatives of the newspaper editors could win.

Football pools coupons were once an extremely popular form of betting in which one had to predict which of each Saturday's football matches would end in a draw. A sizeable jackpot was paid if eight draws were successfully predicted.

During the 1950s, '60s and '70s, the football pools were probably the most common form of betting. Newspapers would advertise such organisations as Copes, Littlewoods and Vernons, who ran the pools. The newspapers would contain articles on the games and give bet suggestions. Radio and television broadcasts would discuss the forthcoming matches and pundits would offer their match predictions.

*

Almost every British household ritually completed the coupon by Wednesday, posted it on Thursday to arrive at the pools office by Friday, in time for the matches on Saturday. Almost every area also had a pools company agent who went from house to house collecting coupons and stakes for a commission.

Some gamblers used this method as it was convenient and the agent saved them the cost of a stamp. But others did not trust the system, believing the agent would keep the stakes and not send the coupons to the pools company. Certainly there were tales of this happening following apparently sizeable wins from someone who had used an agent.

The next part of the ritual for most households (or at least mine) was for dad to find the coupon copy at around 4.30pm each Saturday afternoon. He would then turn the volume up on the radio or, in later years, the television, find a pencil, lick the end of it – I never could work out why dad did this – and tell us kids to be quiet.

The only moment when my young brothers and I were allowed to break our silence was when the announcer would come to the Scottish results. As soon as he said 'Motherwell' and before he could announce the score, we all said in chorus 'yes thanks, how's yours?'. And we all longed for the day when the announcer would declare the result East Fife 5, Forfar 4. Unfortunately it was never to be (although in the 1963-64 season the result came up in reverse: Forfar 5, East Fife 4). Stupid, yes, but it stuck in my mind.

For a few minutes we dream of how we would spend the money if we became millionaires. But by 5pm we would all know the truth, and humdrum normality would return.

Nowadays, with the pool noticeably lower than in years gone by, larger payments are only made if eight score draws are predicted correctly and, compared to the National Lottery, the sums involved are relatively minor.

All these limitations on placing a bet did not apply to those few who could provide bankers' or other credit references. They were able to open telephone credit accounts with the leading bookmakers.

My dad knew all these options and venues like the back of his hand and, apart from credit telephone betting, used them to the full, but with little good fortune and often with dire consequences that would leave mum worrying where the next meal was coming from. Somehow she and dad always managed to rustle up something and to get by until the next drama hit.

*

Despite my father's habits, my first real brush with bookmakers came about thanks to my grandmother. She also lived in Limehouse, in a nearby council flat. Like many housewives of her time she enjoyed a bet and knew how to go about placing one. But as she got older her grandsons, me included, would often run errands for her.

One Saturday when I was still in primary school, and when betting offices were still not legalised, granny asked me to place a bet for her with the local street bookmaker. Granny explained that between 10am and 11am, Monday to Saturday, Charlie the (illegal) bookmaker would be behind the launderette in Harvard Street, a few streets away. It transpired that granny always placed a bet on a Saturday.

She explained that Charlie could easily be recognised as he was the man with a book and pencil in his hand and a flower in his jacket button hole, that there would probably be a group of people talking to him. And he had one leg.

Granny wrote out her selections on a scrap of paper, which invariably included the horses Lester Piggott was riding. Her bet was always a sixpence each-way double and then she would add a third horse, and include this horse for a sixpence each-way treble. She would confirm the total stake by writing 'two shillings' (10p in today's decimal money), at the bottom of the slip, together with her chosen nomme de plume 'mary xx'.

Everyone who placed a bet with a street bookmaker had a nomme de plume, a name either they made up or one given to them by the bookmaker.

So off I went with the two shillings wrapped up in the scrap of paper, as if I was going to the grocer's. I found Charlie standing on his crutches, with his book and pen in hand. Rumour had it that Charlie lost his leg in the war, was invalided out of the Army in early 1940 and had made his living as a bookmaker ever since.

I handed over the little bundle of paper and money, which Charlie took, opened and read before putting the scrap of paper in one pocket and writing a note of the stake and nomme de plume in his book.

This trip to Charlie's on a Saturday became a regular occurrence. Sometimes, not often, Granny told me to tell Charlie that there was money to be paid. But Charlie would not need telling, he would already be looking in his book and counting out money in his hand as I approached. 'Four and nine pence for you my son,' he would say and the money would be handed over with a wink.

One wonders what child psychologists and the child protection service would nowadays make of parents and grandparents letting their offspring roam the streets, putting on bets with illegal bookmakers. But these were much different times.

Over time I got to know and to like Charlie. One day, when I was still about ten, I asked Charlie why he did not get a shop or somewhere to work from. Charlie laughed and explained that what he was doing was not legal and that if the police saw him and caught him he would be in trouble. Seeing Charlie standing on his crutches I figured he wouldn't have much of a chance of running away if police did come down the street and saw Charlie taking bets.

I naively asked Charlie if he wanted me to keep an eye out for him at the entrance to the alley that led to the back of the launderette. Charlie laughed, thought for a bit and said 'You're on my son, whenever you can, that would be great.'

Little did I know that Charlie already had his adult lookouts, two men who stood nearby and doubled up as 'heavies' should any punters get argumentative over a bet. Nevertheless, whenever I spent more than a half an hour or so on a Saturday morning keeping an eye out for patrolling policemen, Charlie would drop sixpence into my hand as he left his pitch.

In any event, the local police would give Charlie adequate notice when his pitch would be raided. There was an informal deal that on each raid police would arrest somebody – anybody – who would then appear in front of the magistrate for slap on the wrist and easily affordable fine. As long as the same person didn't appear in front of the magistrate more than three times there was not too much to worry about. This cosy, albeit rather farcical, arrangement worked well; everybody was happy.

Some neighbourhoods had a street bookmaker who would regularly visit houses, knocking on doors, to see if anybody wanted bets to be placed. It was all an open secret, and no one knows who was kidding who that the law was, or was not, being upheld.

My education during the early years also involved family trips to London's greyhound stadiums – often Hackney and Clapton. What possessed my dad to take me and my brothers to the tracks is not clear, but I suspect it had something to do with children being allowed in free if accompanied by an adult. He would never pass up the chance to get something for nothing.

Greyhound racing stadiums in the 1950s and 60s were noisy, smokey places – full of humorous banter, excitement, joy and sadness in equal measure.

Prince Monolulu was an example of the bizarre humour and interesting social experience that could be found at a greyhound racetrack. I was probably no more than nine when, on one of my regular trips to Hackney Wick stadium, I came across a towering black man dressed in green velvet trousers, a red cummerbund, white silk shirt, gaily coloured waistcoat and a head-dress comprising large, brightly coloured feathers. A binocular case hung around his neck and his attire and accessories were finished off by a hand-held fly swat.

The sight of him left me wide-eyed and speechless, which was

Prince Monolulu.

compounded when he shouted: 'I've gotta horse'. Why he shouted this at a greyhound stadium was, to me, all part of the madness of the scene.

I was later to learn that he was known as Prince Monolulu and his famous catchphrase was 'I've gotta horse'. My dad explained that the man sold tips and for a few pence would share the benefit of his racing knowledge. But it seemed that few had any confidence in those tips as Prince Monolulu was rarely approached.

During the next few years I would often see Prince Monolulu selling his wares at other racetracks, and East London markets such as Petticoat Lane. The Prince was born, not of royal blood of a tribe from Abyssinia as he claimed, but simply Peter Carl Mackay in the Caribbean in 1881. Ever the publicist, he walked alongside (supposedly fellow) royalty at King George VI's funeral. No one bothered to stop him, either for fear of upsetting the proceedings or in the mistaken belief that he was actually from royal blood. Can you imagine this happening today?

In his memoirs Jeffrey Bernard, the humorous racing journalist, claimed to have had some input into the death of Prince Monolulu in 1965. Bernard said he had visited the Prince in the Middlesex hospital where he was recovering from an illness. Bernard had taken a box of Black Magic chocolates for the patient and, in his hospital bed, Monolulu opened the box, chose a strawberry cream and promptly choked to death. As I was to find throughout my career in the betting industry, you could not make it up.

One day my trips to the dog tracks caused me a little embarrassment, when an English teacher explaining some common sayings asked my class: 'what does the expression going to the dogs mean?'. No answer came. For whatever reason, the teacher pressed me to answer. After some careful thought, and with the premonition that my response would not be right, I answered: 'Going to Clapton or Hackney Wick sir'. Shortly after a wooden blackboard eraser went whizzing past my ear.

My favourites were night meetings at Clapton, which opened in 1928 and had an upstairs viewing balcony. Although small, in its heyday the track experienced crowds of 30,000.

At night, at the start of a race, the running track was all that was lit. The moon and stars glistened above and just as the (imitation) hare started its run, a hush descended on the barking dogs in the starting traps. Then whoosh, the hare would sweep past the traps, the gates would fly open, and the crowd would roar in unison and cheer on the dog that was carrying their money.

Starting traps are metal boxes with usually six self-contained sections, with a door at the back and metal grille at the front. Each section is just large enough for a greyhound but tight enough to prevent the dog moving around and possibly end up facing the wrong way. When the hare passes the traps, the starter operates a lever, and the front of the traps (metal grills) fly open in unison.

The six greyhounds burst out, chasing the hare that is already disappearing around the first bend and heading towards the finishing line. The whole race lasts only around 30 seconds.

In greyhound racing the sight of the electronically driven hare motivates the greyhound to run. It travels around the track at a constant speed – one that the pursuing greyhounds can keep up with.

On some tracks the hare is installed on the outside rail, on others it is on the inside. In open races, in which greyhounds from different tracks are invited to take part, the home greyhound generally has an advantage.

Rumours were rife if a greyhound's form improved from one week to the next. Was it 'got at' the previous week? Did the trainer intentionally over-feed it, or give it a stomach full of water just before the race?

Or had the greyhound been 'blooded' before the race, which meant being allowed to catch and kill a live hare as an incentive in its next race to chase what it thinks is the real thing and bring a dramatic improvement in form.

Part of the fun of greyhound racing is convincing yourself that your fancied dog still has a chance of winning, even if it is trailing some lengths behind. Anything can happen in a dog race. Even a dog which is running last at the final bend can get up to win on the finishing line.

After the race, as with all sporting events and betting, those who had backed the winner would shout and jump for joy. Those who had lost would blame others, and other factors, such as their dog had been 'got at'. Although the fixing of races was, and still is, always a possibility, punters always like to blame their misfortune on something other than their own misjudgement.

Research into the psychology of betting has shown (perhaps unsurprisingly) that having a bet, and selecting a winner, produces a pleasurable 'high' in the brain. A gambler is therefore always looking to get a 'hit'. Equally, selecting a loser gives a low that the gambler wants quickly to erase by backing another winner. Hence how compulsive and addictive gambling can become.

Family folklore had it that one day my dad won so much money that he splashed out on a taxi and came home with his pockets stuffed with cash. If this did happen it never repeated itself and the cash was soon spent or, more likely, lost. Fred, if not a compulsive gambler, had the bug.

In later years I would come to appreciate the moral dilemma with which the betting and gambling world wrestles. With alcohol or drugs there is the medical fact that one's body can say 'no more' before shutting down into a drunken unconsciousness or a medicinal 'high'.

With gambling the body does not shut down, the end only comes when there is no more money with which to bet. Fortunately, however, betting is an enjoyable pastime for most and only a rare few suffer addiction.

Certainly the spectacle of horse racing and to some extent greyhound racing, coupled with the buzz of betting, was a great draw for crowds, both before and after the Second World War. One needs no further explanation than to ask where else could prince, pauper and the great mass of people in between achieve such thrilling, live, open-air entertainment.

Racetracks were the only venues where people could legally bet. In a way everyone was equal, all watching the same event and, in the main, sharing the same emotions.

*

I considered that Scurry Gold Cup nights at Clapton were the best. Once a year a carnival atmosphere pervaded the stadium, with free food and drink (lemonade for the children), a grand firework finale and a marching band. The marching band was invariably the Dagenham Girl Pipers.

What a surreal sight the Dagenham Girl Pipers were. Here, at a greyhound stadium in the heart of impoverished East London, was a bunch of local women dressed up as Scottish natives in tartan kilts, sporrans, white blouses, neck ruffs and berets. They would march up and down the inner area of the racetrack, either banging away on marching drums or blowing for all they were worth on bagpipes. Apparently the band was formed by a Congregational minister back in 1930. One can only wonder why.

The Scurry Gold Cup was the major event at Clapton. It was contested over one circuit, 400 yards, of this small track and, for the purists of greyhound racing, the race attracted the best sprinters in the greyhound world. The track closed, with much sadness, in 1974 and the site is now a council housing estate. The Scurry Gold Cup still takes place, but at the Perry Bar greyhound racing stadium in Birmingham.

Apart from the actual racing I found other entertainment in observing the opera that was performed between bookmakers and punters. Bookmakers would stand at their pitches and on their joints shouting out the odds of the dogs, frantically altering their chalkboards as they either took bets or heard of other bets being taken. Punters would be running up and down the bookmakers' line of pitches, trying to get the best odds for the dog they fancied.

26

*

Mini dramas unfolded all the while as punters tried to place bets at advantageous odds, with bookmakers frantically trying to change those odds, attract other bets and balance their books before the race started. This all took place before a backdrop of bookmakers' tic-tac men relaying the latest odds and bets from bookmakers in different parts of the stadium. The secret code of the tic-tac men, who were effortlessly signalling in their white gloves, provided a mystique to the proceedings.

I began to notice two men standing in the same place at each meeting. They would keep a watchful eye on the bookmakers, but would never place a bet and would make furious notes in their books just as the race started. I discovered some years later that these men worked for reporting agencies such as the Exchange Telegraph Company (Extel) and Press Association (PA).

It was their duty to report the starting price (SP) of all of the dogs for each of the races. They would confer after each race and agree what the last price for each dog had been, from a wide sample of the bookmakers at the track. Their findings and conclusions would be printed in the next day's racing papers.

This was an important task, because off-course credit account bets would be settled using the prices returned by these men. Post 1961 the off-course greyhound bets would amount to hundreds of thousands each day, as the sport became a popular betting medium. Consequently these SP reporters needed to be accurate in their findings and men of integrity. A similar scenario was in place for horse racing.

Over time I learnt the slang and signals used by the bookmakers and tic-tac men, something I often put to good use in later years. I could see what type of bets were being hedged by one bookmaker to another, what odds changes were imminent and, using this information, place bets at advantageous odds to get that all-important edge over the bookmakers.

Tic-tac signals and language is akin to cockney rhyming slang, so the verbal code at least came easy to me. Bookmakers would say, for example, lady (Godiva) for a fiver, and cockle (and hen) for ten, and so on. Cockney slang was originally used to confuse and to keep information secret from the police. It was introduced and used from Dickensian times.

In essence the slang often relies on the second (and silent) word rhyming with the subject, so the user needs only to use the first word. Some examples are skin (and blister) for sister, and apples (and pears) for stairs. It is not a dead language but a living and growing one. Some other examples are Ruby (Murray, a singer from the 1950s) for curry, and Nessun (Dorma, the World Cup theme for Italia 90) for stress and trauma.

Other cockney expressions used by bookmakers include: airs (and graces) for races, boracic (lint) for skint, butcher's (hook) for look, nanny (goat) for Tote, dog (and bone) for phone, rabbit (and pork) for talk etc.

*

There was also a purer language exclusive to bookmakers. This normally involves simply reversing the spelling of the word. For example, ten would be pronounced net, four would be ruof, seven would be neves and so on. So, 7-4 (odds of seven to four) would be pronounced as neves to ruof – a jumble of words for the uninitiated, but a meaningful statement for those 'in the know'.

I learnt bookmaker's tic-tac sign language, but with the understanding that part of the code would be reversed or turned upside down by the bookmakers. This was to stop others gaining the inside information. Generally, however, and to give an example: right hand on left wrist is 5-4, right hand to left ear is 6-4, right hand on shoulder is 7-4, both hands on top of head is 9-4, both hands on face is 5-2 and so on. Come the mid 1990s, however, this sign language became useless as bookmakers began to use walkie-talkies and mobile phones. Nowadays, the full sign language code can be viewed by anyone with a simple search on the internet.

The walk up the hill from Clapton stadium to the bus stop was generally quite sombre – full of ifs and buts and conspiracy theories. But the sombre mood did not last long and Fred, with his sons in tow, would invariably cheer up when the 253 bus arrived at the Clapton Pond bus stop. We would all pile on board and head to the crowded top deck – the place for smokers in those days.

One of my dad's first lessons to his sons was: 'When at a crowded bus stop, or any queue for that matter, stick your elbows out, don't let anyone overtake you, and tread heavily on the toes of anyone who tried'. The advice often came in handy.

CHAPTER TWO

LEARNING THE BASICS

Greyhound Stadium Tote Betting,
How To Make a Book, A Settler's Secrets,
Different Types of Bets

One of the most interesting features of greyhound racing to me was the Tote board. This is a huge structure that takes up most of the far end of a greyhound stadium. At night, when the board is lit up, it is a magnificent sight.

The Tote board displays the number of bets that have been put on so it is constantly being updated. It shows how many bets placed in the win pool, place pool and forecast pool (greyhounds to finish first and second). Large enough to be seen by spectators around the stadium, it also has to accommodate details of each of the six greyhounds in the win and place pools as well as the 30 different forecast combinations for any of the six greyhounds to finish first and second.

In the early days the board was mechanical, with numbers printed on large panels that would flip over – with a large clunking sound – as bets were placed.

Nowadays, most Tote boards are electronic, with illuminated numbers replacing the old panels – but still a wonderful sight.

My dad showed me how to calculate the payments that would be made for a win or any one of the 30 forecast possibilities. Stadium owners, who kept the profits from Tote betting, deducted around 20% of the cash bet in each pool. The amount left would then be shared out equally among those with winning tickets.

Knowing that the owners took a share came in useful when betting, because it could be seen if the Tote would pay more or less than the odds being offered by the stadium bookmakers. Though one had to bear in mind that the Tote could change dramatically nearer the race.

Similarly, the odds offered by the stadium bookmakers would also change significantly as the race drew closer, but it was always useful to watch how betting was shaping on the Tote.

On all racetracks, greyhound and horse, I saw how bookmakers competed with the Tote for the punter's pound. Just as the Tote works on a gross profit of around 20%, bookmakers also try to achieve a similar return. The main difference is that the Tote profit is guaranteed, whereas the on- course bookmakers' profit is theoretical.

*

At ten, I started to learn about fractions and percentages, not from my schoolteachers, but from Fred, my dad. He explained it to me thus:

With the toss of a coin there are only two outcomes, heads or tails. The probability of either of these outcomes is equal and in bookmaker parlance the true odds are even money. But, if a bookmaker offered these odds it would be unlikely that he would make a profit as there is no margin in offering odds of even money on what is a two-horse race.

Fred continued that a bookmaker would offer odds of 4-6 in a two-horse race where both possibilities had an equal chance. In this way, in a theoretical book where bets of £60 were place on both horses, the bookmaker would have taken £120. No matter which horse won, the bookmaker would only pay out a total of £100 – a profit of £20 on a turnover of £120. The profit would therefore be 16.6% of turnover and the book is said to be 20% over-round.

This theory, Fred concluded, forms the basis of how odds are first offered by bookmakers of any kind. They will either use their own judgement, or rely on the services of a professional form expert to decide what prices should first be offered. Odds provided by a professional judge of form are referred to as the tissue prices, and these odds will have an in-built profit margin. From there on the weight of money placed via bets will determine the odds that are offered by bookmakers.

My dad considered that only a quick calculation was needed to establish the theoretical profit (over-round) a bookmaker is working to. You just needed to find out how much must be staked on each runner in order for a payout (including the stake) of £100 to be achieved.

So, in a four-horse race, where the odds on offer for the runners are Evens, 6-4, 6-1 and 6-1, then £50 at evens will pay out £100, £40 at 6-4 will pay £100, £14.29 at 6-1 will pay out £100.03. The addition of the four stakes of £50, £40 and £14.29 (twice) comes to £118.58 – an over-round book of 18.58%. With experience, the stake needed to pay out £100 for each of the odds comes to mind automatically.

I wasn't much interested in the lesson at the time but, sensing my lack of interest, dad told me: 'The essence of a shrewd punter is recognising and knowing value in betting'. More importantly, I recognised that, as a bookmaker, it was vital to know if the book had at least a theoretical profit margin.

My father wasn't to know but, in practical terms, the profit margin he had explained to me was always just a theoretical one. Over the ensuing years I would see that bets taken on a race were not evenly spread and in most races there were only ever two or three horses backed with any significance. So often the 'book' was not balanced, and little or no money was ever taken on the middle-order horses and outsiders. Over the years I also discovered that, unlike the Tote, every bookmaker suffers this imbalance.

But it is vital to ensure that there is a theoretical profit margin in the odds offered and that the book is not over-broke (no profit margin). This would happen when, in a three-horse race or even a football match (where there is the possibility of a home win, away win or draw), the odds offered for the three possibilities are 2-1, 2-1 and 3-1.

In this example the stakes needed to pay out £100 on each possibility are £33.33, £33.33 and £25. This gives a total of £91.66 and results in a book being 8.33% over-broke. Given this scenario the sharks (punters who continually look for value) would pounce, as there would be a no-loss situation for them.

This may be too simplistic an example, but there are occasions when if the various odds offered by different bookmakers are compared it can be possible to put oneself into such a no-loss situation. This type of betting is called arbing or arbitraging (more of this in a later chapter).

Coincidentally, my older brother, also named Fred, joined the William Hill organisation a few months after I had joined Ladbrokes. Fred joined Hill's as a trainee settler, in their head office at the Elephant and Castle in South London. Betting ran in the family. Hill's wanted 18-year-olds for these positions and I, being still 16, was ineligible to apply.

I was, however, keen to learn all I could about the business and so I persuaded Fred to show me at night what he had been taught during the day.

There were so many exotic bet types. Not only win and each-way bets and doubles, trebles, and accumulators, but also patents, yankees, canadians, goliaths, fidos, any-to-come, up and down, single stakes about, double stakes about, rounders, roundabouts, flags, union jacks. The list was seemingly endless and all involved multiple selections.

Then there were other types of bets to learn such as forecasts and tricasts, not only in singles but also in doubles, trebles and yankees. Other terms to learn and remember were ante post, stop at a winner, pari-mutuel, Tattersalls' rule 4, dead heats, first-past-the-post betting, bankers in multiple betting, combined odds and so on.

Next brother Fred taught me how to calculate the returns (winnings) from bets – and I thought I was getting into the real secrets of the trade. Remember that we are in the 1960s, before decimalisation, and money was pounds, shillings (20 shillings to the pound) and pence (12 pennies to the shilling). The coinage at this time included the farthing (a quarter of a penny), a half-penny (half of a penny), a penny, a three-penny bit (three pennies), sixpence (six pennies), shilling (12 pennies), two shillings or two bob (24 pennies), two and six or half-a-crown (30 pennies). No wonder people had holes in their pockets!

There were also difficult odds such as 100-9, 100-8, 100-7 and 100-6.

Fred stated the obvious when he told me that anyone can calculate what £5 at even-money is and, given time, £10 at 13-8, but what about when there is a winning treble of 5-4, 7-4 and 4-6?

My brother explained that the first thing a settler needed to learn was the knowledge of 'fraction breakdown'. Most people, when trying to calculate how much they have won for their £10 at 7-4, work on the basis of 'money to money'. For example, £7 is won from the bookmaker for a £4 stake, another £7 is won for another £4 stake and it can be seen that £3.50 is won for a £2 stake. Hence £17.50 is won for a £10 stake. Therefore, and including the £10 stake, a punter will collect £27.50 for £10 on a 7-4 winner.

But there is another way, which is particularly useful when the stake does not easily match the odds, which can often be the case. It is the method that settlers use – fractional breakdown.

Fractional breakdown uses simple steps to get to the winning amount (7) from the stake amount (4). So, using 7-4 as an example, to get to 7 from 4 one takes the simple steps of once, plus half, plus half, ie 4+2+1=7. In betting terms, and to include the stake in the returns, one must think: evens + half + half. So £10 on a 7-4 winner would be calculated as £10+£10+£5+£2.50 = £27.50. £14 on a 7-4 winner would be £14+£14+£7+£3.50 = £38.50.

And to show how using the settler's fractional breakdown method is better than the money-to-money system used by the normal punter, Fred asked to me try to calculate a £5 double on two 7-4 winners using money-to-money. Compare this to the fractional breakdown method thus: £5 on 7-4 = £5+£5+£2.50+£1.25=£13.75. Then £13.75 on 7-4 = £13.75+£13.75+£6.87+£3.44= £37.81. Easy!

Fred gave me the full list of the breakdown for odds, a sample is given here:

4-9 = stake + third + third (eg £10 at 4-9 = £10+£3.33+£3.33 = £16.66)

4-7 = stake +half + seventh (eg £10 at 4-7 = £10+£5+£0.71= £15.71)

4-6 = stake + half + third (eg £10 at 4-6 = £10+£5+£1.67 = £16.67)

4-5 = evens – fifth

5-4 = evens + quarter

11-8 = evens + quarter + half

6-4 = evens + half

13-8 = Evens + half + quarter (eg £10 at 13-8 = £10+£10+£5+£1.25 = £26.25)

15-8 = 2-1 – eighth (of stake) (eg £10 at 15-8 = £10+£20-£1.25 = £28.75)

Fred told me to memorise these formulas, but that they could be figured out if forgotten. He explained that the same method is also used for calculating place bets eg £10 on a 6-4 placed selection at fifth the odds is stake + fifth, ie £10 + £5 = £15.

The next stage of my basic education into the secrets of the bookmaking industry, or at least the betting office and credit department side of the business, was how to calculate the exotic bets. These had been thought up in an effort to encourage punters to try for big wins from relatively small stakes. Bookmakers referred to these as 'mug bets', on the basis that they were a great profit earner and generally it was only mugs who placed them.

They were also offered as an alternative to the on-course bets available such as the Tote double, Tote treble and in later years the Tote Jackpot and Placepot. Many punters were aware of doubles and trebles, even the illusive winning multi-selection accumulator. But now there were yankees, patents, roundabouts, rounders and union jacks – to name just a few.

As in every trade the professional has ways of making the job look, and be, effortless – betting office and credit department settlers are no different.

Fred gave me the following example: Take a £1 winning yankee with four winners. A yankee being four selections, in 11 bets, comprising six doubles, four trebles and an accumulator. You could work out each of the 11 bets separately and, after maybe an hour at it, having used copious reams of paper, come up with an answer. But Fred explained the 'block' and 'crash block' methods to me – by laying the bet out as I have done below, and the use of a few calculations.

BLOCK METHOD

As an example, using four winners, all winning at even money, this is what a £1 block yankee graph would look like. The block method is used when the individual totals for doubles, trebles and accumulator are needed.

		db	tr	ac	total
evens	£2				
evens	£2	£4*			
evens	£2	£8**	£8		
evens		£12	£24	£16	
		£24	£32	£16	**£72**

CRASH BLOCK METHOD

Using the same four winners, this is what a £1 crash block yankee graph would look like. The crash block method is used when only the total return is needed.

evens	£2*	
evens	£2	£4**
evens	£2	£16***
evens		£52
Total	**£72**	

In essence, £1 (the unit stake) is put on to the even-money winners. Then the calculations are progressed thus:

In the block method the first £2 is put on to the second even-money winner with the result of £4* and this is put under the first double column*. Then the total of the first two even-money winners (£2+£2=£4) is put onto the third even-money winner, with the result of £8** and this is put under the second double column, and so on. This process is repeated throughout the graph.

In the crash block method, after £1 (the unit stake) is put on to the even-money winners, the first £2* is put on to the second even-money winner, which results in a return of £4**. Then this £4, plus the sums from the first two even-money winners (total of £8) is put on to the third even-money winner. This gives a return of £16*** and so on. This process is repeated throughout the rest of the graph.

Obviously the two totals are the same, but the block method shows the separate figures for doubles, trebles and the accumulator, and thus how the grand total is reached.

The explanation, when written down, may seem complicated, but in practice, both methods are simple and straightforward. And Fred explained that I would come to rely on them – the block method was used for multiple doubles and trebles etc, not only for win bets but also for each-way bets where the selections had finished in the frame. And, surprisingly, yankee bets do often have at least some return.

It was interesting – and somewhat surprising – to learn of these complicated and involved mathematical processes which I am sure would defeat even the most accomplished maths teacher. One of my other brothers is a maths teacher, and one day I would like to confront him with this and see how he copes with it. But the settlers in the back rooms of bookmakers' establishments up and down the land would in those days make light work of this.

CHAPTER THREE

THE EARLY 1960S AND THE REALITY OF BETTING SHOPS

Betting Shops Legalised, How To Obtain a Betting Shop Licence,
Horserace Betting Levy, Telephone Credit Betting, First Job In
A Betting Shop, Hedging, Clock Bags- Runners-Factory Agents,
Old School Bookmaker-Protection, Internal Fraud, Rigged
Football Match, Dagenham Coup, Sleepers.

So the story of 50 years of betting shops, and my time in the betting
industry that runs parallel, begins.

The Sporting Life's story on 1 May 1961 ran: 'Cash betting is now
legal in shops. Off-the-course cash betting becomes legal in Britain
today. If you have a fancy at Nottingham, Lanark, Wye or Hexham you
can go to a betting shop, pay over your stake money and receive your
winnings in cash immediately after the weigh-in, just as if you were
actually on the racecourse.'

Most years have their memorable and historical moments and
1961 certainly had its fair share. Among other events the farthing (a
quarter of an old penny) ceased to be a coin of legal tender. Amnesty
International was formed and the Berlin Wall appeared. Mothercare
started and the romance between the Ken and Barbie dolls began. The
satirical magazine *Private Eye* hit the streets. Ernest Hemingway died
of self-inflicted gun wounds and John F Kennedy was inaugurated as
president of the USA.

The biggest event in the UK was undoubtedly the licensing and
legalisation of betting offices, ending the farce, or at least most of it,
that had gone before.

*

The process for opening a Licensed Betting Office was fourfold. First
the proprietor (bookmaker) needed to acquire a bookmaker's permit

The Sporting Life *from 1st May 1961, proclaiming the new legalisation and, as of that day, allowing the opening of betting shops.*

from the local magistrates' court. In later years this was granted to those who, among other criteria, could show good character and were relatively financially secure. But in the early 1960s a 'good character' could sometimes be a liability in obtaining a permit. Some magistrates, hearing applications for a bookmaker's permit, would ask the applicant 'have you run an illegal book?'. If the answer was yes, the permit would be granted, along with a warning that the bookmaker should trade legally in the future. If the answer was 'no' then often the permit would be refused because the applicant did not have the relevant experience.

The next stage was to find premises that had normal office facilities and somewhere for the punter to be served. A crunch point was the location as the local licensing authority had to agree there was a need for a Licensed Betting Office; this was otherwise known as 'the demand test'.

A landlord also had to be persuaded to grant a lease to a bookmaker, and in the early days this was not always easy so many bookmakers preferred to buy the freehold.

The third stage was to obtain planning permission from the relevant department of the local council – which was again no easy feat in those early days.

The last hurdle was applying for a license for the premises in open court, where the bookmaker had to persuade the local licensing magistrate of the suitability of the premises, its layout, whether there was demand for the business. Representations from the local community were all considered, too.

The government's rationale in passing the legislation that allowed betting shops was that curbing illegal betting had proved unworkable. But even though Licensed Betting Offices were now allowed, the government still wanted to discourage betting among the masses and tried to keep the new betting offices out of the public eye.

*

By the end of May 1961, the first month after legalisation, there were approximately 7,000 betting shops open and trading. By the end of 1962 there were over 13,000 and by the end of the 1960s there were more than 14,000 betting shops open.

The horse racing lobby of the time was, as now, an influential one, and insiders feared that attendances at racecourses would decrease with the opening of betting shops. As a consequence they convinced the government that betting shops should pay a levy to the horse racing authorities on horse racing bets that were taken in the betting shops.

Winston Churchill had tried to impose such a levy on bookmakers in 1926, but the bookmakers of the day would have none of it and to show their discontent they had gone on strike at Windsor racecourse and withdrew their services. Without bookmakers to bet with, the race-going public showed the government their displeasure and the levy idea was soon dropped.

Things were different in 1961. Betting shop operators were grateful they could now trade legally and there was a willingness to contribute to the sport that provided their core business. The first levy was based, with some provisos, on either 10% of profit, or 0.25% of turnover, whichever produced the greater figure. It was estimated that it would bring in approximately £1million. In the event it raised just under £900,000.

The second levy scheme was a charge per shop, dependent upon turnover. On the scale of charges the middle range was £600 per shop, but although this was the middle of the scale it was not the average turnover – which just over £200 by the end of the 1960s. Nevertheless, the total amount raised annually increased steadily during the decade and by 1969 it had reached just under £2.5million.

The levy is renegotiated each year. The statute book declared that if the bookmakers and the Horserace Betting Levy Board (HBLB) could not agree on a scheme in any particular year then the Government, by order of a minister, would decide on the scheme and rate of contribution. It may come as no surprise to learn that, apart from those years when a pre-arranged deal had been incorporated from a previous year's agreement, the first levy scheme was the only levy when a minister was not called in to determine the scheme.

It is strange that this new industry, which would bring employment, tax contributions, and benefit to the horse racing industry through the levy, had legislation applied to it that resulted in Licensed Betting Offices becoming basic and soulless places. Legally, there could be no advertising on the premises, no inducement or encouragement to bet, no seats, no drinks or refreshments, no radio or television broadcasts, and opening hours exclude Sundays and periods after 6.30pm.

*

The Government's intention was that punters go into the betting office, place the bet or receive payment, and come straight out again. The legislation demanded that no passer-by should be allowed to see inside the premises so as to remove temptation of casual trade. That is why, until the early 1990s, the windows of Licensed Betting Offices were painted over and the front doors were always kept closed or had tatty coloured strips of plastic hanging from the door frame.

One might wonder what the locals made of the titles that were displayed over the betting premises. 'Betting Shop', 'Licensed Betting Office', may be clear and descriptive enough, but what were they to make of 'Commission Agent' or 'SP Office' or more confusing still 'Turf Accountant'. There were surely cases of bewildered gardeners entering Turf Accountants, wanting to buy grass seed or turf.

Ever since they opened, Licensed Betting Offices have had something of an identity crisis. What were they, offices or shops? The public began to call them, and to recognise them, as betting shops. Yet legislation did not allow them to operate as a shop.

This confusion lasted for many years. Over time, betting office owners wanted to be recognised as operating shops and be part of the retail, or even the leisure scene, on the high street and to be able to attract the leisure pound of the potential customer.

At the outset, however, betting offices were drab places. Inside would be an area where the public, standing on a plain wooden or lino floor, could read the pages of *The Sporting Life* or *Daily Mirror* and write out their bets. In this area, or behind the counter, would be an area where a large blackboard would be displayed. An initially unemotional broadcast by the Exchange Telegraph (Extel) company relayed the day's race results into the betting offices.

The blackboard was used, and in some betting offices it is still in use, to display results, along with racing and sporting event information. The person who worked this display was called the boardman, an integral part of the operation, who would often turn his board into an art form.

First, one had to clean the blackboard with wet old newspapers to give it a better surface to work on (because the black printers' ink from the newspaper rubbed off on to the board). Then, as the results were being announced they would be written using wet and different coloured chalks. The wet chalk would give the display more depth as it dried on the board, and the different colours would provide impact and clarity, for the winning horse, favourite, SP, and Tote dividends.

A good boardman would display all the information on the board: not only the results but also jockey changes, non runners, weighed-in announcements and, vitally important, not miss any of the price changes that were broadcast, by Extel, from the courses.

*

Some punters would favour a betting shop because of the boardman. This was not only because of his ability but also his personality. The board was usually in the customer area of the shop and he would often banter with the customers.

In time, chalk would give way to felt marker pens and handwritten lists of runners would give way to printed sheets. These sheets were produced by a company called Jackson and Lowe, that also produced settlers' marker sheets and wall-display form guides for greyhound racing. And as TV screens have taken over the provision of results and shows displays, and racing papers such as *The Sporting Life* and *Racing Post* provided marker sheets for settlers, the use of Jackson and Lowe in betting shops has diminished.

The counter would be a work surface plus maybe a 2ft high metal or wooden grill, behind which stood the settler – normally the bookmaker proprietor – and depending on how busy the office was, a cashier or cashiers.

Basic equipment on the counter would be a timing machine and a pack of two-part numbered and coded tickets.

The timing machine would stamp on to the betting slip the time the bet was taken. Then one ticket of the two-part numbered tickets would be handed to the punter. The other, carrying the same number, would be stapled to the actual betting slip.

The number of the ticket and the stake paid would be handwritten into a ledger. In later years this process would be replaced by the use of a till.

When tills were introduced the slip would be passed through it. These early versions would simply stamp a number on to the betting slip and issue the same numbered ticket for the betting slip. This ticket would also show the stake money received and it would be handed to the customer in exchange for the bet stake money.

The betting slip, used by the punter, would be anything from the back of a fag packet to a piece of writing paper.

Depending on how seriously the proprietor took security and record keeping, some form of microfilm camera might also be in use. These microfilm cameras came in many designs, the early ones being of a glass, flat-top design and would be fitted into the counter. All bets taken could then be placed on the glass to activate the camera to take a picture, and permanent record, of the bet. The camera would also record the exact time the bet was taken. It had, as with all bookmaker microfilm and other bet-acceptance systems up to the modern day, an inbuilt self-contained, independently powered clock.

*

Some of the early betting shop operators tried to continue trading as they did on the street corner. Stories abound of punters walking into a betting shop, passing a slip across the counter, or even through a hatch back then, and being asked for their nomme de plume. With this written on the slip the transaction would be completed.

Fraud, arguments over late bets, payment of winnings to the wrong customers, tax and company record requirements soon encouraged these early operators to become more professional.

My experiences at Ladbrokes gave me one valuable insight: as a telephone credit bookmaker, you have to win the money twice. With any form of credit betting the bookmaker not only has to win the bet, but also has to then get the credit account customer to pay for the losing bet. It was often a difficult feat as some, maybe understandably, would not want to pay for something knowing there would be no gain. I witnessed many account holders who, if they suffered a bad run of fortune, seemed to disappear and leave their accounts dormant and in arrears, never to be seen or heard from again.

This insight would stand me in good stead in years to come when, in advising bookmakers, the attractive option appeared to be to expand the credit facilities and let the customer have whatever bet they wanted – dangerous philosophies in the bookmaking business. Some years later, the phrase 'turnover is vanity, profit is sanity, cash is reality' was coined. Never a truer saying.

In 1964, after nearly two years with Ladbrokes, I moved to work as a trainee settler with a bookmaker who had two betting offices in North Woolwich, Silvertown, in the docklands of East London. I was 17, and was to spend six interesting years with this organisation, Mike Connor Ltd (Connor's). The owner Cornelius Eggerty (known as Con, not necessarily a great name for a bookmaker) and his general manager Albert Perry taught me all I needed to know about bookmaking, and of betting shops in particular.

As I was not allowed inside the actual betting office until I turned 18, I was put to work on the telephone in the rear office of the main shop in Silvertown Way. Connor's had a busy telephone credit account business. My duties included taking bets from customers over the phone and writing them down on individually numbered pads.

Even in those days, this entrepreneurial bookmaker had an MBO (Management by Objectives) and PI (Performance Indicator) measurement for his staff. He demanded the phone be answered within two rings and with the greeting 'good morning' or 'good afternoon M Connor Ltd', that the caller be addressed as 'Sir' or 'Madam', the bet should be taken professionally and read back clearly. Also, the total stakes of the bets had to be instantly calculated and read back to the customer.

In addition a type of settling efficiency, quality control and security was achieved as Albert would ensure that any overnight bets still to be paid in the shops, or via agents and phone accounts, were checked and re-settled by another settler. Con would check bets on the microfilm camera himself to ensure they had been placed in time, and that after the result was known there were no subsequent additions or alterations on the slip.

I was also responsible for settling the phone bets and for informing

Albert if any of the multiple bets were running up, ie had winners and would possibly win a large sum for the customer should all the selections be successful. This vigilance was vital as it allowed Albert to judge whether or not he should hedge some of the bet.

*

Most members of the public believe that bookmakers are guaranteed to win money and, if a bookmaker has a large bet to pay out, they would have hedged it anyway. The truth is rather different. Hedging is fine if perhaps a large bet has been taken in an effort to provide a punter with the bet that he wants – in which case the bookmaker will lay some or all of it off (hedge it/place the identical bet) with another bookmaker. Often the larger bookmaker will give a small commission to the smaller one who is giving the bet away.

It was also the case that, if a punter placed a bet with Connor's on horse A to win the Derby at 4-1, Connor's may be able to find another bookmaker who would give him 9-2. Thus, Con the owner or Albert the manager could decide if the whole bet should be given away (hedged). This would produce a profit should the horse win (Connor paying £500 to the customer, but receiving £550 from the bookmaker where the bet was hedged). Or, only hedging perhaps £91 of the £100 bet. Thus ensuring a guaranteed profit of £9, no matter what happened. Should the horse win the customer would receive £500, but Connor's would also receive £500.50 from the bookmaker where the bet was hedged. Should the horse lose Connor Ltd would have the customer's £100 in the bank, yet only receive a bill, from the other bookmaker, of £91.

But, I discovered, Connor's need to hedge was in bets such as yankees and other accumulator-types. A simple example I recall was when a punter had placed a £2 fivefold accumulator. The first selection won at 2-1, no problem, the second won at 2-1, still no problem, the third won at 10-1. The other two selections were both showing at 6-1. Thus the customer had £198 going on to the next two horses for a potential final return of a little short of £10,000 – a small fortune in those days.

Although Connor's, as with all small independent bookmakers, had varying limits, and on five-horse accumulators 'down-the-card' it was 2,500-1, so a little comfort there, but still a potential payment of £5,000.

The expression 'down-the-card' refers to selections that run sequentially, with gaps of at least 20 minutes or more between the off-times of races. That is opposed to the expression 'across-the-card' where the selections run in races that are off at either the same time or are less than 20 minutes apart.

Bookmakers and betting office owners had, and some still do have, differing limits for accumulator type bets. Where the selections are classed as across-the-card the payout limit will be much smaller than if the selections are down-the-card. This is because a bookmaker will have less time to take possible hedging action should the across-the-card selections be winners.

Everyone in the office was involved in the problem of what to do with this £2 fivefold. If a (double) bet of £198 was placed on the last two horses, and one of them lost, there would be a bill for £198 from the bookmaker with whom the bet was placed, but there would be only £2 (the stake) from the customer. If nothing was done and the two horses won the customer would be in for his £5,000 win for his £2 stake.

*

As is often the case, a compromise position was decided upon as the right choice. A £75 double was placed on the last two horses, which would return £3,675. With something of a sigh all round from Connor Ltd, neither of the horses won. The customer lost £2, and Connor's received a bill for £75, so were £73 out of pocket on the bet. But if the last two horses had won, Connor's would have been £1,325 down on the bet. That was a manageable amount but not something the business could sustain every day.

I speculated about what I would have done if it had been my business. What would have been the right thing to do? Maybe jump in and hedge sooner on the bet, possibly before the 10-1 chance had won? Hindsight is a wonderful thing.

This type of dilemma presented itself many times to Connor's and to many other small betting office operators over the coming years. Nowhere were there any textbooks to advise on the best course of action. Over time I saw that, for the independent bookmaker, gut feeling, instinct, experience, knowledge of the sport involved in the bet and shrewdness were the only guides.

I soon discovered that Connor's, and its proprietor Con and manager Albert, were real old school bookmakers. First there was the wage process. I was offered a more than generous salary but I was often suspicious that what I was receiving did not match the National Insurance and tax contributions that Connor's were supposedly paying on my behalf.

I also noticed that Con employed two maintenance handymen, Dickie and Roger. When it came to painting and plumbing, however, they were both a bit of a disaster. But over time, and looking at their size and the way they carried themselves, it became obvious that their purpose was more troubleshooting or debt rather than maintenance. Con's large Alsatian dog, who accompanied him everywhere, completed the scene.

Times have changed since those early days and not many operators now need assistance for their personal protection. But back in the 1960s the criminal element did try to muscle in, offering 'protection' for betting shops and, if they met with a refusal from the owner, a few windows may be smashed or a fire might be started in the shop. Danny Quastel had a small group of shops in South and East London and at least one was set alight. In Soho, a bomb blew up on the opening day for another betting shop. Over time however, and despite the unfortunate and persisting public perception, the criminal element was discouraged and eradicated.

I saw that Con also had 'runners' and factory agents. The runners and agents were something of a hangover from the old pre-betting shop days, but nevertheless still something of a profitable hangover for all concerned. The runners were based in the numerous pubs scattered around the area, availing themselves to the local populace would knew they would take bets and place them with Con. It saved a walk to the betting shop for the pub regulars.

*

The agents worked in the various industries in the area. These included the massive Tate and Lyle sugar refinery, Rank Hovis McDougal bakery, the Amoco oil refinery and the Royal Docks. These firms had many employees who either could not, or were too lazy to, get out of their place of work to put on their bets. Even with betting shops now legal on the high street, agents were still doing good business in some areas, Silvertown being one of them.

Agents and runners would receive 6d (2.5%) in the pound commission for every bet they collected for Connor's. There was no risk for the agents or runners, Connor's took all the risk. The agents and runners used the clock-bag system. Clock bags were leather pouches made from a whole piece of leather, with no stitching or joins, sized something between a large purse and a small handbag.

A vitally important part of the bag was the metal, box-like contraption the size of a cigarette box that was used to close and securely lock it. When the bag needed to be closed and secured, the top of it would be inserted into the metal box and the holes at the top of the bag would be lined up with metal bolts in the locking mechanism of the box. When all was lined up a small lever on the box could be activated, the metal bolts would lock into place and the bag would be secured.

The metal box also had built into it a small, wind-up, accurate stopwatch. Once the bag had been locked into the box and the lever activated, the stopwatch would start to run. Before the first race, when the bets taken were due to start, all the betting slips would be put into the bag and the bag locked into the metal box.

Back at the office, knowing that often the bag containing the bets would arrive there after racing had ended, Con or Albert would calculate how long the stopwatch had been running. Then they would satisfy themselves that the bag had been locked into the box before the first race. Using a unique key, the box would be unlocked, the bets taken from the bag and settled by Con or Albert.

Many of the agents and runners had more than one bag. In this way they could take bets up until the time that the first race of the day had started. But, should other bets be offered, these could also be taken and put in the clock bags before the relevant races started.

Throughout the late afternoon and early evening runners and agents would turn up at the main office in Silvertown Way and hand in their clock bags. Later in the evening Con's son Mike would drive around the factories in which Con had agents working night shifts to collect the clock bags. Mike would return to the main office, unlock the bags and immediately pass the bets through the glass flat-top microfilm camera. The bets would then be handed to whoever was doing the 'dog duty' that night. Very rarely would Mike delegate this job, but if he did he would stand by and watch the bets being photographed before counting them and noting the number.

The 'dog duty' was the 6.30pm to 10.00pm shift, when one member of staff would stay behind at the main office, answering the phone and taking bets for the greyhound races run that night. The results would come in and the bets would be taken over the phone, plus those taken in the two shops during the day and from agents and runners bets would be settled. The results would arrive from the Exchange Telegraph Company via a ticker-tape printer. Think of those old 1950s Hollywood movies about Wall Street and newspaper rooms where ticker-tape machines would be whirling way, with maybe a newspaper editor or Wall Street investor, cigar in mouth, busily scanning the tape for the latest news flashes. That was the type of ticker-tape machine Con had.

I learnt that payout limits for the bets in the clock bags were much lower than other bets Connor's accepted, because Connor's would only be able to open the bag to see the bets after all had started. Most of the races on the bets would have finished by the time the bag was opened, so Connor's would not be aware of the liabilities of the bets and unable to hedge them.

If occasionally short of staff, Con would employ someone he knew to cover the dog duty shift. Soon after I joined there was one such occasion – which had an interesting conclusion.

Tim was a retired dock worker. He used to be a tally clerk – somebody who kept a note and checked the number of boxes, crates and sacks of goods that were unloaded from the ships. Tim knew his racing and how to calculate basic bets, and was forever pestering Con for a job in the betting shop. One day he was offered some dog duty shifts, and having jumped at the chance, he learnt the ropes within a short space of time and would be called upon whenever needed.

However, one morning following a 'dog duty' shift by Tim, Albert saw that a punter of one of the factory agents had won £100. This was from a £5 win double bet on two greyhounds that had won at odds of 4-1 and 3-1 in two 7.45pm races the previous evening. There was another £5 losing double on the bet.

Tim rang Albert that morning, explaining that as the winning bet was on races across the card he had no opportunity to hedge any of it. Albert saw that the punter's nom de plume was a new one and the agent had been with Con for under a year.

Smelling a rat, Albert arranged for the microfilm in the camera to be developed. Later that day he and Con sat down to view the film. It was no surprise to either that although the winning slip was found on the film, the part that contained the winning double had Tim's massive thumb covering the bit where the winning selections should be. It was obvious that no selections had been written on the part hidden by Tim's thumb. Con arranged to meet Tim and took Dickie and Roger, his 'maintenance men', with him.

To cut a long story short Con discovered that the agent had approached Tim to carry out the fraud. The plan was for Tim – if ever he was given the bets to photocopy on the microfilm – to put a slip in to the bundle of bets and to photocopy it, but at the same time ensure that not all the bet could be seen. Then it would be a simple task to write out a winning bet on the slip once the results were known and to put it in with the rest of the bundle of betting slips from the bag. The winnings would be split between the agent and Tim.

But the pair failed to consider how many years Albert had spent in the business, and the dodgy bet stood out a mile to him. Police were not involved on that occasion, but the maintenance men may have had some fun coaxing out the truth from Tim.

Once this episode had settled down Albert would tell me of stories from times gone by. He believed that the public always thought the bookmaker to be the villain. So if Tim had not admitted to what he had done, and because of Con's suspicions, the bet would not have been paid, and there was no doubt the agent would have broadcast that Connor's were welching on a bet.

Albert explained that this distrust of bookmakers was longstanding. For instance, when there was suspicion that a race or event had been fixed the public always believed the bookmaking fraternity to be at the bottom of any skulduggery. But in reality it was often the bookmakers who suffered from the skulduggery. On top of that, the betting public who were not in on the fix were also cheated when a race or event was fixed or rigged.

Albert relayed the story of football match fixing. The fixing had been exposed in the newspapers earlier that year (1964), just before I was employed at Connor's. Sheffield Wednesday player Jimmy Gauld sold his story to the papers of how he and three other players fixed a game that Wednesday had played against Ipswich in 1962. He said Sheffield Wednesday had deliberately lost the game because those players had placed bets on Ipswich to win. At least one bet of £50 was involved. Not exactly a king's ransom.

But Gauld's efforts to raise money backfired on him. All four players, including Gauld, were charged with varying offences. Gauld was charged and found guilty of conspiracy to defraud, and was sentenced to four years imprisonment.

Another example, from June 1964, was an episode that became known as the 'Dagenham coup'. In essence a large gang went around the country placing forecast bets on the four favourite greyhounds in a race at Dagenham greyhound stadium that evening. Just before the race, the gang plus others involved in the coup, more than 90 of them, met at the stadium. As the Tote windows opened for the race in question, members of the gang stood at the windows, slowly placing forecast bets. Nearly all of these bets included the two outsiders in the race.

The intention was to stop other ordinary race goers from placing Tote forecast bets. Their plan worked. The gang placed just one forecast bet on the favourite greyhounds, filling the Tote pool with money on the outsiders and with only one bet registered for the forecast favourites.

The race was run, the second favourite beat the third favourite and the Tote dividend for the correct forecast was a massive, in today's coinage, £987.55 for a 10p stake, or 9,874-1. There was just one winning ticket on the stadium Tote – one that had been placed by the gang.

So, although the money wagered on the Tote, on the outsiders, was lost, the gang held many winning bets that they had placed earlier in the day in betting shops. It was estimated that off-course bookmaker's liabilities ran into millions, maybe in excess of £20million.

Albert said that the bookmakers' trade organisation took the matter to court in an effort to make the race null and void. The bookmakers took out a writ accusing the stadium of unlawful conspiracy to defraud bookmakers. This was in addition to and despite the fact that there was no legal obligation for the bookmakers to make payment. Seeing that public opinion was against them, however, and being a new industry, the bookmakers were keen to be seen to be acting properly.

The judge did not uphold the allegation of conspiracy to defraud, but he did state that the purpose of Tote betting was to allow those who wanted to place a bet to be able to do so, and therefore those who had bet at Tote odds off-course should receive payments that reflected the odds produced by those that wanted to place a bet on-course. Because this did not happen on the night in question at Dagenham, and because members of the public were stopped from placing bets on the Tote, the judge ruled that the race was void. The off-course bookmaking industry breathed a sigh of relief.

Albert was trying to explain that the betting public themselves were responsible for the events being fixed. And the object of the exercise? To ensure the perpetrators could either steal money, or at least obtain it unfairly, from the bookmakers.

But back on the legitimate side of the business, the first Prix de l'Arc De Triomphe I had to deal with at Connor's came as something of a surprise. There was something Fred had neglected to tell me about pari-mutuel betting. Although, in some quarters, pari-mutuel returns have come to mean most foreign racing Tote dividend payments, there is another facet to the pari-mutuel return in France.

In France, where there is only Tote (pari-mutuel) betting and no bookmakers, it is accepted that when a bet is placed on a horse, if the owner has another runner in the race the bet will be coupled with the owner's other horse for betting purposes. As Michael Caine would probably have said: 'Not a lot of people know that', or at least did not know it at the time.

*

Time and time again, while working at Connor's, I was asked by punters who had backed the winner why the pari-mutuel return was so much less then the bookmakers' ante-post price. The answer lay in the fact that, in pari-mutuel betting, although the punter may not have wanted it, his bet was also getting the benefit of being included with the owner's other horse. And, more importantly, those that had bet on this other (losing) horse would be paid out as a winner. Thus the payout dividend was lessened, as it had to include those bets on the owner's other (albeit losing) horse.

Conversely, those that had bet on the winning owner's losing horse often did not know, or realise, that their (losing) bet had become a winner, due to the French pari-mutuel coupled-horses proviso. Therein is a problem for the industry that, to this day, still has not been resolved. It has become known as the 'sleepers' issue.

Sleepers are bets that have money to be paid on them but, for various reasons, the punter who owns the bet has failed to make a claim. Often the simple reason why the bet has gone uncollected is that the bet is indeed a loser, and the settler, or settling system, has made an error in the calculation or event result.

Working behind the counter I could not fail to notice there were, and still are, times when there is money to be paid on a bet but the customer is unaware of it. It could be that the bet was taken late, after the designated 'off-time' of the event and was made void but, if the selection did not win, the customer would assume the bet was a loser. And there the void money would sit, in the bookmakers' tills.

Many bookmakers, Connor's included, shared these unpaid sleepers out among the staff, which was a great perk and was one reason why Con and Albert had a procedure of rechecking any bets still to be paid after 24 hours. Other betting shops, particularly the large multiples, would bank the money as unclaimed debts.

A sleeper could also be caused by a customer seeing his horse lose, throwing his ticket away and walking out of the betting shop. The punter would not know that a stewards' enquiry or a jockey's objection was about to be announced and his horse promoted to first place, would turn his bet into a winning one. Again the winnings from the bet would just sit in the bookmaker's accounts or be paid to staff.

The issue of sleepers remains a controversial topic. Many pundits and politicians raise the subject of what should happen to bets remained unpaid. There is a call for bookmakers to pay these sums into racing, racing charities, or to sports bodies or sports charities. Whose money is it? Not the bookmakers' say some. In response, the bookmakers say that the money belongs to the customer and, as the customer can make a claim for the money at any time, the money should not be given away to a third party.

*

Bookmakers often retort that money from sleepers goes some way to making up for those occasions when customers may be overpaid because of errors by staff. Though they would not object to donating a small percentage to a good cause, a minority of bookmakers openly state that any money not collected by customers is a perk, given the ancillary taxes and levies placed on them that are, in their view, mostly inequitable and unwarranted.

Some betting shops have tried to address the issue by displaying bet receipt numbers at their counters for bets that have been made void or that remain uncollected. Rarely, others might even advertise unpaid bets in the local press.

Whatever the course of action, the debate over what to do with uncollected monies rages on.

CHAPTER FOUR

THE LATE 1960S

East London Shop Management, Football Betting,
Punter Cons, John Banks Licence To Print Money,
Betting Tax- Betting Duty Book, John Pegley, Foinavon,
Foot and Mouth, Mullingar Favourites,
Jeffrey Bernard,

Connor's was a relatively small, family business and the employees were a well-paid, tightly knit group. Most betting shop employees were well paid at the time and the industry was difficult to get into. So it was something of a surprise when the manager of one of Connor's two shops announced his departure to one of the larger companies.

Betting shops had been open for four years and this was the first time Con had to find a new manager. Placing an advert in *The Sporting Life* (the *Racing Post* of its day) seemed the best way forward. However, I had another solution, and suggested to Con and Albert that, though just 18, I should be the replacement shop manager.

I felt I had proved my worth to Connor's, putting to good use what my brother and Albert had taught me. Maybe Con and Albert thought 'better the devil you know', but they duly confirmed my appointment as possibly one of the youngest managers of a betting shop.

The shop I managed was not a difficult one. Two experienced cashiers were employed at the branch, barely a mile from Connor's main shop and head office at Silvertown Way. Albert was only a phone call away and Con Eggerty would often pop in should a problem arise. The customers were, in the main, genuine, local, old-fashioned, honest East End dock workers and, in any event, Dickie and Roger the 'maintenance men' were just five minutes away should there be any trouble.

In later years I would look back at some of the things I had to deal with during my three years as manager of that shop and think: 'what a time, what a bunch of people'.

The first big event I remember was actually a non-event from a betting perspective. This was when England won the Football World Cup in 1966. Obviously this was a major cause for countrywide celebration, especially in the East End of London where the West Ham trio of Geoff Hurst, Bobby Moore and Martin Peters were instrumental in England winning the trophy. But, and it is somewhat unbelievable to think of it now, England winning the World Cup did not even appear on the betting radar of the time.

Back then, betting on football was mainly confined to the pools. The days of large-scale, in-play, fixed-odds match betting, and fixed-odds first goal scorer betting and all the other possibilities was to come.

*

One of the reasons why football was not part of the betting shop scene in 1966 was because in 1964 the government had imposed a fixed-odds football betting tax of 25% on stakes. Before this, betting on football had been huge – in 1963 it was put at £65million. The bets were placed by post, and both Ladbrokes and William Hill had a large operation in London to deal with them.

The bets would be the multiple-selection, fixed-odds type in which a customer would be guaranteed a certain return – for example five away wins or three draws. The tax, introduced in 1964, virtually killed off betting on football using odds and many bookmakers closed this part of their business. In 1966 some of the major players, notably Ladbrokes and William Hill, came back to the market and tried to make a go of betting on multi-selection football, offering fixed odds.

They were partially successful. But then, in 1968, the tax was raised to 33.3%. Certainly the football pools people must have been quite influential at this time, as they once again feared any success by bookmakers on football betting would be detrimental to pools betting. In 1972 this tax was again raised to 42%, putting an end to this type of betting.

Every cloud has a silver lining though, and it was perhaps just as well this tax had been introduced, and killed off this part of the industry by 1966. If not, and betting on football was not restricted to multiple-type bets, many a bookmaker would have gone out of business because of the England victory.

I also remember, with some amusement, some of the tricks and cons that punters at the shop would attempt. Greyhound forecast doubles and trebles were very popular at the time.

In the 1960s, indeed even up until the 1980s, there were still many greyhound stadiums in and around London which held evening meetings twice or sometimes three times a week. The popular bet of the day for a normal eight-race card was a set of trap numbers such as one and two, or five and six, for a bet of 28 straight forecast doubles, or 112 reverse forecast doubles. Often Wembley and Wimbledon stadiums would race on the same night. This is when the sharks would come out. Picking busy times of the day in the betting shop, the sharks would try to get their bet taken past the cashier. The bet would read 28 forecast doubles traps one and two at Wimbley. Or 28 forecast doubles traps one and two at Wembleydon.

When written by hand, the ambiguity of whether the bet was for Wembley or Wimbledon was assured. The following day, the punter would come in claiming that the race meeting intended was for whichever stadium had produced the best results for the bet. Thus ensued the weekly argument between me – and no doubt many other betting shop managers – and customers.

There were other avenues for punters to write ambiguous bets. These included trap or horse race numbers where a three could be written so that it looked like a five or an eight, a one that could look like a seven, a six that could look like a zero, so 16 could be 10. The obvious purpose of writing an ambiguous bet was to attempt to get two bites of the cherry – two bets for the price of one – providing the punter could convince the betting shop manager that the instruction interpretation was genuine.

*

Another con was the practise of placing late bets, where the result was already known. The time on the till clock would often be a good guide or, if needed, the clock on the microfilm camera. Other common occurrences were forged notes, short changing, understaking bets, attempts to get paid on a bet (with the proper bet receipt) where the bet had already been paid because the punter had claimed to have lost his receipt. Never a dull moment!

And equally not many quiet moments in the industry in general. Just as today, in the 1960s the activities of on-course bookmakers would be reported in the racing press. There was one on-course bookmaker who was causing something of a stir with his larger-than-life personality, driving around in a yellow Rolls-Royce, wearing his trademark large black fedora and making headline-grabbing pronouncements. His name was John Banks, a bookmaker from Scotland, and he was not unlike a Barry Dennis figure today.

Banks had a reputation for laying any bet offered to him and was not just surviving but seemingly thriving in the cut and thrust of the betting ring. His main method of making a book, similar to that of some bookmakers nowadays, was to find fancied runners, decide if they could be beaten and, if so, oppose them by offering longer odds than those offered by other on-course bookmakers. He would keep laying the horse, and hold the price, despite attemps by off-course bookmakers to shorten the price.

Banks also had a string of betting offices in Scotland and became renowned for the saying 'betting shops are money factories and a licence to print money'. In fact his full quote from *The Sporting Life* was: 'I don't call them betting shops, I call them money factories. To have one is to have a licence to steal money. Week in, week out, it just pours in.'

Someone in the Treasury must have been reading *The Sporting Life* that day. In the following year, 1966, the government introduced a betting tax – of 2.5 pence in the pound for every bet placed. In 1968 this was raised to 5% and in 1970 to 6%. By 1974 this tax was up to 7.5%, reaching a peak in 1991 when it was 8% of turnover. I often wondered if John Banks regretted his outburst.

Politicians considered other ways of raising taxes from betting shop owners. One that came under consideration in the late 1960s was a tax based on the rateable value of a betting shop. However, one Portsmouth-based bookmaker, John Pegley, took up the fight against it. He rode up and down Whitehall on a bike, bearing the message 'never seen a bookie on a bike? Now you have'. He and fellow bookmakers, acted as pall-bearers, carrying coffins around the streets outside Parliament with the message: 'Rateable Value Tax Will Kill Off The High Street Betting Shop'. The publicity worked and the tax soon became a non-starter.

When the betting tax was introduced, Con, my employer, who had a business consisting of two betting shops, a telephone-credit business and a network of agents, just shrugged his shoulders. He was a wily old guy and had been one of the first licensed betting operators to receive a permit to open for business in May 1961.

*

He had been truthful in declaring to the licence-issuing magistrate that he had previously been operating illegally. Con knew he would get a bit of a talking to but he figured that if he said he had not been operating as a street bookmaker then a licence would not have been granted.

Maybe John Banks was right, maybe betting shops were money factories. Certainly from what I saw as a (by then) 19-year-old manager, profits were good and relatively easy to come by. Little did I know of Con's plan to ensure the tax had less impact.

For smaller organisations like Connor's the tax had to be paid in advance. The following month's turnover had to be estimated and a cheque for 2.5% of this had to be sent off to HM Revenue and Customs (HMRC) prior to the start of the month. A record of the estimated turnover, the tax paid, and the actual turnover had to be kept. The BD (Betting Duty) book was born.

This book would prove useful in years to come when betting shops were bought or sold. The BD book would become the major piece of evidence that would confirm the turnover of any betting shop; largely determining the shop's value.

Betting shops were advertised in various ways, most often in *The Sporting Life* or a monthly magazine called *The Licensed Betting Office Proprietor*, which was full of interesting articles and news about the industry. One regular feature that I liked to read, as no doubt did all other managers and settlers in the business, was a piece by The Professor. Each month it would cover ways of simply and quickly calculating some of the more exotic bets that were proving popular with customers. Although some of the articles covered the bet-calculation short cuts I had already learnt, they were always an invaluable read.

The magazine sadly ceased publication in the 1970s, when its proprietor/editor died. After a while its place was more than adequately taken by the excellent publication *Bookmakers Office Supplies* (BOS), but unfortunately the articles by The Professor ceased.

So, what of Con's plan to ensure the newly introduced tax would have minimal effect on the business? Although I could never be sure, I had a suspicion that bets taken by his network of runners and agents, plus the other bets taken over the phone, went undisclosed to the taxman. So a large part of Connor's turnover would escape the 2.5% tax. Con couldn't get out of his old school ways.

*

It was common knowledge that tax inspectors visited betting shops, placing 'test bets' which would be followed up on subsequent visits to the premises. On these visits the tax inspector would ask to see the record of his bet and would then check against the records to ensure that his and other bets had been registered accurately and the correct amount of betting tax paid.

With the runners, agents and phone bets, however, these were an unknown part of the business for the inspectors and one in which they could not place test bets.

Carnage at The 1967 Grand National, in which Foinavon won from the back of the field.

In those halcyon days it was also an open secret that a bookmaker could put fictitious 'winning' bets through his books. This would have the effect of reducing the annual profit and therefore the corporation tax to be paid. I have no doubt that those old school operators used this type of skullduggery if they had an exceptionally good year.

One such year was 1967, when Foinavon, ridden by John Buckingham, won the Grand National. Foinavon won biggest betting race of the year at odds of 100-1. It was not so much that he won the National, more that the others lost it.

The horse was a genuine no-hoper, but this actually helped him to win the race. On the second circuit, with Foinavon at the back of the field and the leading horses about to jump the 23rd fence, the one after Becher's Brook, a riderless horse – ironically called Popham Down – was at the front of the pack.

Popham Down had fallen at the first fence, got up and carried on without his jockey. But Popham Down decided the 23rd would be one obstacle he would not jump; and refused before running across the front of the fence. This caused the horses following him to either pull up or tumble into the fence. More horses and jockeys coming up from behind saw the carnage ahead and pulled up; some stopped so abruptly they threw their riders over the fence.

John Buckingham, on Foinavon, saw the scene in front of him but because he was so far in arrears he was able to steer Foinavon around the mayhem and successfully jump the fence. He then stole a long lead, which he maintained to the finishing line (the remarkable pile-up is there for all to see in video footage on the web). The Tote return of 444-1 was probably an accurate reflection of Foinavon's true chance of winning the race.

Foinavon had been named after a group of mountain peaks in Scotland (the word is Gaelic for White Mountain). If you visit Aintree and walk the Grand National course you will see that alongside the famous fences Becher's, Valentine's and the Chair, the 23rd fence has been named Foinavon. This is not because of the mountain-like difficulty in getting over it – as it is one of the smallest on the course – but after the horse who provided the Grand National with such a sensational result. Maybe it should have been called Popham Down after the horse that caused such mayhem; it has a more obvious meaning to it, don't you think?

I spent most of that 1967 Grand National day putting my settler's red pen through 99% of the bets taken on the race. A few had placed the odd shilling (5p) each-way on Foinavon, but the result was almost a skinner for the book. It was celebrations at Connor's that day with a bonus and, later that evening, beers all round for the staff.

*

But there was a shock coming for betting shop operators later that year, in what turned out to be one of the worst periods for bookmaking for a long time to come.

In October 1967, just before my 20thbirthday, news broke that a sow on a farm in Shropshire had foot-and mouth-disease. I thought no more of it and carried on managing my shop. But over the coming days I began to realise that what had happened on that farm in Shropshire was serious. Horse racing was cancelled and no animals were allowed to move out of the area that they were already in. Over the course of six months 430,000 animals were slaughtered in an effort to eradicate the disease. Many farmers lost their livelihoods.

Picture the scene in betting shops up and down Britain with no horse racing for many months. Some Irish and French racing was covered, as was greyhound racing, but turnover was in the basement. This event and the subsequent bad weather winters of 1967/68 and 1968/69, when racing was abandoned for several weeks at a time, were catastrophic for betting shops. Most let go of some or even all of their staff, or put them on reduced hours. Some went out of business, while others sold up for a pittance to the larger organisations.

So, although it was clear that owning a betting shop could produce a good living, profit was by no means assured. Industry leader Cyril Stein of Ladbrokes saw the long-term potential of betting shops and bought up and opened as many as he could. By 1967 he had 109 premises, and five years later more than 1,100 betting shops had the name of Ladbrokes above the door.

Likewise the William Hill organisation. In the early days the organisation, taking a steer from William Hill himself, did not see betting shops were a profitable long-term option. William Hill the man loathed their very notion and was quoted as saying betting shops were 'a cancer on society'. But in 1966, when it was clear what profits were being made, the William Hill organisation, somewhat belatedly, also started buying up shops from those proprietors who wanted out.

Both the Ladbrokes and William Hill organisations, as well as some other enlightened bookmaking entrepreneurs, sent their managers to scour the country looking for crowded betting shops with the aim of applying for a licence to set up a competing shop in the vicinity.

*

This was of course long before the 2005 Gambling Act so the 'demand' test governing where a shop could be opened was still in force. Top lawyers were employed and, despite objections from the existing local independent bookmakers, the licences were, more often than not, granted on the grounds that existing demand was not being met.

But back to the 1967 foot-and-mouth outbreak. Con did not even think of selling. He kept all his staff and weathered the storm. He knew how to treat his staff and that he would need them when normality returned.

When racing resumed, I noticed that some of the regulars failed to return to the shop to place bets. It was a pattern I saw reoccur in years to come whenever racing was abandoned for any length of time due to bad weather or the like. It made me consider the psychology of the punter and in my somewhat amateurish way I reached the conclusion that, just like any addict, if a regular gambler can be weaned off their addiction they will be more able to resist the urge to partake should temptation be put in their way again.

The other strong reason to resist taking up the habit again is the cost. Just as when smokers give up, when a punter stops betting, even if it is enforced, they would be discouraged from starting again after seeing how much better off they are financially.

Touching on addictive behaviour, compulsive reading for anybody interested in betting were Jeffrey Bernard's columns in *Sporting Life* and *Spectator*. His column in the *Spectator*, Low Life, was a reflection of his own life as a habitué of down-at-heel Soho. Bernard's passions were cigarettes, horse-racing, women and drinking. Each day he would drink a minimum of a bottle of vodka and smoke 60 cigarettes, he was a compulsive punter and illegal bookmaker in equal measure, married four times and had countless other liaisons.

Bernard's writing was full of irreverent wit, insight and vivid description of the dramas and larger-than-life characters, many from the world of racing, whom he came across. It was compulsive reading. His biographer, Graham Lord, said of Bernard: 'He had many wives, four of them were his own'. When contemplating writing his autobiography Bernard placed an advert in the newspapers which read: 'I would be grateful to any readers who could tell me what I was

Jeffrey Bernard outside his favourite pub in the Coach and Horses in London's Soho.

doing between 1960 and 1974'.

As a writer for *The Sporting Life*, Bernard was given a free pass to every racecourse and he used it with enthusiasm. Long days at the races, long nights on the tiles and an attachment to the vodka bottle meant he was frequently incapable of filing any words and would miss his column deadline. On these occasions a line would appear where his column should have been, which read: 'Jeffrey Bernard is unwell'. It became the title of a successful stage play about Bernard's life, written by Keith Waterhouse. Because of his unreliability, Bernard was sacked from *The Sporting Life* in the early 1970s, but rejoined some years later only to be sacked again. He died in 1997 at the age of 65 and his writing wit is sadly missed.

CHAPTER FIVE

THE 1970S

Moving On, Decimalisation, Henry Cooper v Joe Bugner,
Betting shop Procedure, Mecca Bookmakers, Horserace Tote,
Betting shop Workers Union, BOLA/ABB,
Miners' Strike/Three-Day Week, Football Betting,
Greyhound Results by Tennis Balls,
Coups: Gay Future,-Barney Curley and Yellow Sam,
Rochester Greyhound Stadium, In The Money,
Betting Shop Doors Glued Up, John Banks,
Cyril Stein, Totegate, Red Rum, John McCririck.

After managing Connor's betting shops for five years, during which time I learnt about bookmaking as well as the 'shady' side of the business, I felt my career was a little stymied and needed a new challenge. I decided to move on, wanting to progress my career with a larger organisation.

In the early 1970s there were over 14,000 betting shops in the UK – the figure having peaked at just over 15,000 in 1968.

So there was no shortage of choice and I soon got a job as a relief manager with the South London firm Gus Ashe, which had over 40 premises mainly in and around the Camberwell area. The owner, Derek Ashe, had just bought a chain of shops in the Poplar and Whitechapel areas of East London. They offered me an increase in wages and a career path with more opportunities. But it was with a great deal of sadness that I said goodbye to Con, Albert and the others at Connor's.

Although, in most ways, a more enlightened organisation, Gus Ashe was still struggling to get into the full swing of professionalism. Surprisingly, some aspects of Ashe's management and organisational style were inferior to Connor's, most strikingly that the shops had no safes. Thus we managers had to walk the streets, transporting the day's

71

takings to and from home and keeping the cash as safe as possible overnight. It was a state of affairs almost certainly replicated in other small-to-medium-size betting shop organisations.

I managed all Gus Ashe's shops in the East End, from Aldgate and Whitechapel Road down to Burdett Road in Poplar. What a group of shops, from quiet dives to madhouse busy. The quality of the staff matched the diversity of the shops, making the task of managing quite different to Connor's. Now I was aware that I had to be on my guard, not only for punters trying to pull a fast one but also, unfortunately, for staff trying scams.

Alarm bells rang the first time I managed the shop in Whitechapel Road, three weeks after I started with Gus Ashe. Its permanent cashier Ted could, and often did manage the branch on quiet days when there was no horse racing. But on busy days the shop needed a manager who could settle bets quickly and accurately.

As the afternoon progressed I came across a £1 each-way bet (£2 stake) that had been taken by Ted but registered on the till as only £1. Ashe's tills required the betting slip to be put into the till aperture, then, when the cashier had registered the amount of stake and pressed the 'register' button, the till would issue a ticket to the customer. It would also stamp the bet number and the stake registered on to the betting slip.

When I saw only £1 registered on the slip for a bet that was clearly £2 I said nothing, deciding to see how things progressed during the afternoon. Maybe the customer had only given £1 to Ted? The bet lost. I tried to keep a watchful eye on the counter. I then saw a customer put £2 on the counter and place another bet with Ted. When the bet was put across to me it was another £1 each-way bet but was registered as only £1. I then knew that Ted was intentionally under-ringing – one of the oldest tricks in the book and one favoured by staff in public house and retail areas.

The same customer came to the counter again and the same thing happened. This time the bet was a winner. I pointed it out to Ted who said he thought the bet was for £1 (the total stakes box had not been filled in by the customer and Ted said that in the rush he just saw the £1 instruction) but that he now remembered taking £2 from the customer and that the bet should be treated as a £2 bet. I said no more, giving the impression I had accepted what Ted had said. The punter was paid his correct money.

After the shop closed and the staff had left, I stayed behind and went through the bets from previous weeks. Time and again I came across bets that had been under-rung, when either a relief manager had been in charge of the branch or Ted himself. I concluded that Ted thought it too risky to under-ring bets when the regular manager was in the shop, but took the chance when he managed the shop himself, or when there was a new or relief manager.

*

That evening 1 got on the phone to head office. I knew a senior manager or director would be on duty, overseeing the night greyhound business.

I saw no more of Ted and later learnt that Ted had been asked to report to the main office in Camberwell the following morning, where he was instantly dismissed. I never found out if the police were involved.

So an early lesson learnt; where there is money involved one's fellow workers are not to be completely relied upon. In times to come I was often criticised for being distrustful and told 'staff should trust each other; it's all about team work'. I took the same approach as President Nixon did when dealing with nuclear disarmament. Apparently Nixon was asked by a Russian delegate:'Why should there be inspectors visiting each other's countries, don't you Americans trust us Russians?' Nixon replied: 'of course I trust you, but I would like to verify'. Trust but verify, not a bad ethos when dealing with the unknown or untested.

This is not to say that I had little great regard for my fellow staff, who worked in insalubrious surroundings, under constant pressure and often dealing with unruly, aggressive punters. There was always the potential threat of an armed or violent robbery or other attack.

Recognising that the future lay in betting shops, my brother Fred had left the head office of William Hill and also joined Gus Ashe to manage the shop in Old Montague Street, Whitechapel. One evening l received a call from the cashier there telling me Fred had been attacked and the shop robbed.

This was before betting shop fitters had heard of such initiatives as 'designing out crime' –whereby the shop can be set out in a way that made it difficult to carry out a robbery, with the use of wide-angle mirrors, no blind spots, CCTV systems, staff facilities behind the counter, adequate counter screens and so on.

Staff at the Old Montague Street shop had to leave the counter area and walk across the shop floor to get to the toilet facilities. The robbers had waited for Fred to do this and, without warning, hit him on the head with a brick, forced their way into the counter area and stolen the relatively small amount of cash that was available. Fred was rushed to hospital.

Fred did not return to Ashe's, but instead carved out another career for himself in management accounts. Like many other good betting shop employees, he waved goodbye to the industry due to an awful experience.

By the end of 1970 shops were busier and more profitable than ever. Betting tax had been raised to 6% but Coral, Ladbrokes, William Hill and others, including City Tote, were expanding at a rate of knots, either acquiring licences to open new branches or buying existing shops.

*

After just a year I felt I gone as far as I could with Gus Ashe. The local area manager, who had control of the shops in East London, showed no sign of leaving. Having proved I could cope away from Connor's and already at the top of the betting shop manager wage scale at Ashe's, I decided to move on.

Early in 1971 City Tote placed an advert for shop managers in *The*

Sporting Life. I knew that, although trading under the banner of a rather unexciting name, City Tote was a go-ahead organisation. They had a shop not far away from one of the Connor's outlets in Silvertown and it was always a struggle to attract punters away from their shop into ours. I also knew from the industry grapevine that City Tote managers were well paid and earned a commission of 10% of the net profit of the shop they managed.

The City Tote shops were well fitted out, some with carpets. They had dispensed with the old blackboards and had instead installed bright, white, plastic, wipe-clean display boards, on which results were displayed using coloured felt pens. They also allowed their punters to take the latest show price from the course if requested, something of a novelty in those days. Their bet-acceptance system involved a two-part carbonised betting slip, whereby the customer would receive an exact copy of his bet as a receipt. Plus they had safes, or fridges as they were often referred to. No longer would there be a need to carry around large wads of cash. At last my family and I could sleep easily at night, without hundreds, sometimes thousands, of pounds under the mattress, sums which I was expected to guard with my life.

City Tote had been taken over by a global plc, then known as Grand Metropolitan Hotels (now known as Diageo). Grand Metropolitan had also taken over the leisure giant Mecca, an organisation at the forefront of the dancing, clubs, casino and bingo industries.

I responded to the advert and was given one of their shop manager roles. City Tote had a high representation of shops in the East End and West End of London. They also had a run of shops all along the Harrow Road in northwest London, from the Edgware Road to Wembley and beyond.

I was sent to the massive flagship shop at King's Cross to learn the City Tote ropes. This branch had a huge floor area and stood on a corner site right outside King's Cross Station, busy every day of the week. There was a manager, deputy manager, four cashiers and two settlers. There were also two boardmen, one of whom doubled up as a bouncer. While one had responsibility for displaying the latest prices broadcast from the racecourse, the other had responsibility for displaying results and for evicting drunks – and there were plenty of them around, then and probably still now.

Some of the drunks arrived in the shop sober but over the course of the afternoon, using the subterfuge of the ubiquitous vodka bottle in a brown paper bag, gradually lost their sobriety. They would take some convincing that drinking alcohol on the premises was not allowed and it was an everyday battle for the bouncer, who earned every penny of his wages. In most other shops the manager would deal with such issues but at the King's Cross the problem required an ongoing, full-time solution.

It was at about this time that the industry came to terms with the death, at 68 years of age, of William Hill, who had retired in 1970. The William Hill business was soon to be sold to the Sears Holding Group.

I, meanwhile, spent some weeks as a relief manager in the City Tote shops in Oxford Street, Greek Street and Wardour Street in the West End and at various shops in the East End.

After a month or so I was allocated my own shop, back in my East London roots of Roman Road, Bethnal Green. The shop was on the corner of Vallance Road, home of the notorious Kray twins. The Krays never caused problems in any of the shops I worked in, though some of their henchmen used the shops for the odd bet. Some of the shop's cashiers were also girlfriends to these guys, which may be why there was never any aggravation from that quarter.

It was while I was managing the City Tote shop in Bethnal Green that a seismic change occurred in Britain that had a huge effect on the country – the decimalisation of the monetary system and coinage on 15th February 1971. It was called D day, with the D standing for decimalisation.

Instead of having 12 pennies to the shilling, and 20 shillings (240 pennies) to the pound, with a total of seven coins in usage, there was to be a simpler system based on 100 new pennies to the pound. Some of the old coinage would remain for a while, with the old shilling (12 old pennies) now worth, and to be called, five new pence. The old two bob, or two shilling, piece (24 old pennies) was now worth, and was to be called, 10 new pence.

It came the time when, with the tills converted, most of those directly involved with serving the public were ready. But some, if not most, members of the public refused to adopt the new ways. It was as if all the costly government advertising had gone right over their heads. The great British punting public believed their way of life was being threatened and fought against the change. It was either that, or punters just couldn't be bothered to deal with the new situation.

My experience of punters' reluctance to change was that they still came in with their two shilling (10 pence) each-way double bet, total stake of four shillings (20 pence), already written out. My shop cashiers and I would serve the customers with an 'ok that's a 10 pence each-way double, total stake of 20 pence, here's how you write it out for tomorrow and the future' only to be greeted with: 'Twenty pence, what are you talking about? My bet is for four shillings'.

It was the same when winning bets were paid out. Five pence each-way on a 4-1 winner had a return of 35 pence. 'There you are sir, 35 pence,' would receive a response of: 'What are you talking about, I want seven shillings'. When the 35 pence was put on the counter, albeit in the form of three 10 new pence and one five new pence coins (three two shilling coins and one shilling coin) there was usually a grump and a response of: 'That's right, that's what I told you, seven shillings'.

It was easy to see the reason for the confusion. When cashiers used the new terminology the customers perceived that their cash had been devalued. As there were 2.4 old pennies to every new penny, when a winning bet was said to have a payment of, for example, 35 pence (seven shillings or 84 pence in old money) the reaction was probably understandable. It would be similar nowadays if a new pound was introduced which was equal to £2.40 of the old pound.

Some say the introduction of decimalisation was the main cause of the rampant inflation that the UK went through at this time. One should bear in mind that items were a lot cheaper in the early 1970s, and five shillings (60 old pennies) or 25 new pence was of some worth. Therefore one could see how consumers could be lulled into a false impression when they were being told in shops: 'Thank you, that will be 75 pence', whereas previously the cost was 15 shillings or 180 old pence.

Though there were some diehards for a few years, eventually the (new) penny dropped and the public started to use the new phraseology.

Certainly decimalisation made the betting shop settler's job much easier. Most settlers were proud of their prowess – not just their accuracy in calculating winnings but, just as importantly, the speed at which they could get through a pile of bets. I considered myself a top-class settler and senior management started to notice my ability, hence my rapid promotion through the grades of shop manager at City Tote.

This may be the point at which to describe what went on behind the betting shop counter from the early 1970s until the introduction of the EPoS (electronic point of sale) system 30 years later. In some betting shops, EPoS has still not darkened the door and the process that I am about to be explain still exists.

After arriving at the shop, and possibly picking up the racing papers on the way, the manager would keep his fingers crossed that the cleaner had already been to clear away the wreckage from the day before. Failing this he would have to do a quick tidy-up himself. The tills would be totalled to ensure nothing untoward had been entered overnight. The microfilm camera and other equipment such as the television display screens, would be checked to make sure all was working.

Then the safe was opened and the money checked. Cash floats would then be allocated to the tills and the banking for the day (or cheque withdrawal to get back to the shop cash float) calculated and put to one side. Next, the racing papers would be displayed on the shop walls and the shop door opened.

Most betting shops used the two-part carbonised betting-slip method for their customers. This meant that when the customer wrote out a bet, a copy of what was written on the top part of the slip would automatically be replicated on to the underneath carbonised slip. The two-part slip would be handed across the counter to the cashier who would try to recognise the total stake on the slip. Although there was a total-stake box on the slip that the punter should fill in, this was often left blank. The bet would be placed in an aperture in the till, the stake value would be registered in the till and the 'register' button pressed. This would automatically cause the till to produce details of the date, time, till code and amount of cash received for the bet to be stamped on to the top copy of the slip. These details would also be repeated, because of the carbonated slips, on to the bottom copy slip.

The money would be taken from the punter and, as a receipt, the bottom carbonised slip would be handed to the punter. Immediately the top copy would be placed into a microfilm camera machine. This would accept the betting slip and, via a set of rollers, ensure that the slip passed through the machine, photograph it, and then desposit the slip on to a tray at the bottom of the machine. The camera machine would have an independently powered clock inside it. When the camera photographed the betting slip a picture would also be taken of the clock.

*

The cashier would tell the manager of any large bets taken and, for some large stakes, would question whether it was in order to take the bet. More often than not the manager would contact head office for permission to accept any large stake bets.

Efficient managers and settlers would also try to look at each bet soon after it was taken. This was to see if the bets conformed to the company rules and to check that it had been written correctly. Good managers would know that it was better to try to stop bet queries, such as badly written instructions and selections, or incorrect timings, before the customer came to the counter for his winnings. If the manager found a problem the punter could be called to the counter and the bet clarified before the bet started.

At least at the start of each race, if not before, the manager or settler would take the bets from the camera tray and go through them. Then, at the start of the race, the manager would tell the cashiers to process an 'off' slip for the race. Using the bet serial number printed on the 'off' slip from the till, and knowing that future bets taken on the till would have a higher number than that printed on the 'off' slip, it could be used if there was any doubt whether a bet had been placed in time and before the start of a race.

Once the day's racing had started the settler would invariably have his head down at his desk, marking the results on his sheet and ploughing through the pile of bets taken. Some good managers and settlers could boast that their shop took, and that they could settle, 1,000 bets a day. In addition they could manage the punters and ensure the shop was run properly. I considered that I was in this category.

The settler would put a red line through the selection if it was a loser, or mark the price of the selection on the slip if it was successful. Once the selections had run any returns would be calculated and the betting slip given to the cashier for the customer to be paid.

At the end of the day the till would be totalled, the bets paid out would be added up and this paid-out sum would be deducted from the 'take'. This, plus the starting float, should be how much was left in the shop.

In between all this there would be issues to deal with: punters claiming they had been short changed, or that their bet had been settled incorrectly; boardmen missing some results or a broadcast of prices from the course; results being delayed or altered because of stewards' enquiries or objections; messages from head office about suspicious bets or persons to watch out for; calls from other shop managers asking if their calculation on a bet could be checked; or a drunk or some other scallywag to be evicted. Then there was the banking to do and small coinage to be obtained or there might be a message from a cashier or boardman saying they would not be in which brought the prospect of trying to run the shop with a shortage of staff that day.

Then there was the possibility of a till or camera breaking down; or the area or shop suffering an electricity power cut; the chance that the shop might run out of money due to bad results; and the need to keep up to date with the settlement of bets in order to see which were liable to have large winnings on them and would require a phone call to head office. These were all part of the rich tapestry of everyday betting shop life.

*

While on the subject of results, the way punters would react to a bad result for the bookmaker has always tickled me. During every race there would be the inexplicable phenomenon of all the shop punters staring at the board display where the prices for the race had been on show, or at the Extel speaker through which the race broadcast would be relayed. Many would be shouting and cheering on their horse. It was a strange sight. Then, when the horse that most in the shop had bet on, crossed the line first. A roar would go up and the punters would turn to the staff and, with a cheer and arms raised, shout as if they had just won a battle against those behind the counter.

Certainly, most punters do seem to have the notion that the money they hand over the counter to pay for a bet goes straight into the staff's pocket. The majority of punters apparently perceive that it is a battle between them and the staff. Little do they realise that, apart from their own possible personal interest, the staff generally could not care less who wins a race.

Betting is, of course, one of those financial transactions where the customer potentially receives nothing tangible in return. Little wonder they feel bad when backing a loser, yet they always come back for more.

I enjoyed managing the Bethnal Green shop for 12 months, partly because of one particular bet I took on big boxing match between Henry Cooper, the ever popular British champion of the day, and the young contender Joe Bugner.

Henry Cooper and Joe Bugner after their title bout.

Cooper was the long odds-on favourite and had previously, with his renowned ''enry's 'ammer' of a left hook, famously floored the seemingly invincible Muhammad Ali (then known as Cassius Clay). Unfortunately the knockdown happened right at the end of a round and the bell saved Ali from being counted out. Ali's cornermen then contrived to have Ali's glove cut open, thus wasting precious seconds during rounds allowing their man to recover.

Angelo Dundee, Ali's trainer, blatantly and against the rules used smelling salts to revive Ali from his stupor. Cooper subsequently lost the fight, as Ali was able to land punches on the British boxer's 'Achilles heel' above his eye, where his skin was prone to suffer cuts. The fight was stopped with blood pouring from Cooper's eyebrows.

Joe Bugner, although no Ali, was extremely able and well built but he had a questionable attitude – sometimes seeming to lack aggression in fights.

City Tote, as with other bookmakers, were offering odds on the fight's outcome. On the evening of the fight a punter I had never seen before asked if he could place £6,000 to win on Cooper. The odds offered were 1-3 – giving the customer £2,000 winnings and a total payout of £8,000 (less tax) if his £6,000 bet was successful. Head office was contacted and, yes, the bet would be taken.

The customer left without placing the bet but about 15 minutes later, just before I was to close the shop for the day, he returned. He appeared very nervous and hesitant, but asked again if the bet would be taken. I told him it would, and out of his pockets came the £6,000. Who knows where the money had come from? Maybe he had borrowed it and planned to repay it the next day, maybe it was his life savings.

*

Certainly it appeared that he was trying to buy money, an expression used when it is perceived that a punter is using an event where the outcome is thought to be a certainty to increase his capital. Obviously the odds will be very short, but this is of no consequence to the punter, as he thinks the outcome certain. Thus a large sum of money will be placed in the belief that a small win will be achieved, even guaranteed. As many have found to their cost this is a dangerous game to play.

The bet was placed; the first bet over £5,000 I had taken and, for a cash bet, a very large sum of money in those days. So I listened to the fight, which was being broadcast on the radio that night, with great interest. Up for grabs were the British, European and Commonwealth titles that Cooper held. The fight went the full distance and afterwards Cooper went over to the referee, Harry Gibbs, in order for him to raise Cooper's hand in victory. Gibbs ignored Cooper, walked past him and instead raised Bugner's hand.

Cooper and his trainer, known as 'The Bishop', were stunned. Most in the crowd were astonished as they were convinced Cooper had won, and the celebrated commentator Harry Carpenter exclaimed: 'How can they take away a man's titles like that?' when he saw what Gibbs had done. Controversy over the decision continued for weeks, but the result remained unchanged. Of course it was not only Cooper and 'The Bishop' who were gutted, there was also a punter wandering around Bethnal Green £6000 poorer.

Remembering that I was on 10% of net profit, and knowing that the shop had already earned enough to cover the expenses for the financial year, I thus earned £600 on the bet. At the end of the year I received a gross commission salary bonus payment of just over £1,000 as the shop had performed well overall. Not a bad sum for those days.

There have been many other bets since in which I have had direct involvement, with cash stakes – and I do not exaggerate – of hundreds of thousands of pounds. At such times the biggest concern as is how to keep the cash safe. Banks do not welcome payments in cash of large sums of £100,000 or more. 'Can you give us a few days warning?' is a normal response from the head cashier.

Henry Cooper and his manager retired from boxing soon after the fight, stating that it was partly in protest at the referee's decision. In later years Cooper would be involved in promoting boxing, believing it was a worthwhile sport in which to take part.

Boxing however has its critics. One from that era was Baroness Edith Summerskill, who was in favour of its abolishment. In an interview with Cooper, she pointed out the brutalities of the sport and asked him: 'Mr Cooper, have you looked in the mirror lately and seen the state of your nose?' Cooper replied: 'Well madam, have you looked in the mirror and seen the state of your nose? Boxing is my excuse. What's yours?'

*

Some 40 years after the Cooper v Bugner fight, on 1 May 2011, the 50th anniversary of the legalisation of betting shops, Cooper died at the age of 76. Sir Henry Cooper OBE, a true British legend will be remembered by those who had the good fortune to meet him (outside the ring, that is) as a self-effacing gentleman who, despite his fame and achievements, never lost the common touch.

During the year 1972 I moved to a larger shop in Clapton, just up the road from the old greyhound stadium, and it brought back many childhood memories. It was also the year that the Tote belatedly got into betting shop ownership. Set up by Winston Churchill in 1928 under the title of the Racecourse Betting Control Board (RBCB), the Tote was retained under government ownership. Unlike the Tote at greyhound stadiums, from which the profits are kept by the stadium owners, the Tote that operates at horse race meetings is governed by the Horserace Totalisator Board with the duty of ploughing its profits back into horse racing. Given that it has a monopoly of providing pool betting to racecourses producing a profit should not be too difficult but in some years, it did seem an unobtainable goal for the organisation.

Totesport, the name by which the Tote eventually operated its 500 or so betting shops, was rather stymied when it was first launched as it could only take bets on horse racing. But its shops were soon allowed to take bets on other sports and in 1997 it was finally allowed to compete on an equal footing with bookmaker competitors when it was allowed to take bets on any event, including numbers betting.

Mainly due to the need to raise money for the Treasury, the Tote, including Totesport betting shops, was sold off by the government to Betfred bookmakers in 2011 for £265million, despite having been priced at £400million when a sale was first considered several years ago.

Betfred, based in Warrington and previously known as Done Bookmakers, gained a reputation through large-scale advertising of being 'the bonus king'. It famously paid out bets early on Manchester United winning football's Premier League (Fred Done is a long-time Manchester United fan), only to see Arsenal grab the title. The company started in Salford in 1967 with just one shop and had 840 before the purchase of the Tote. Betfred is also credited with inventing the popular Lucky 15 bet in 1984.

I would imagine that it was little comfort for the group's employees at their head offices when Betfred announced that redundancies would

Fred Done.

be kept to fewer than 150. Say it quickly and 150 seems a small enough figure but for those left without work, with families and mortgages, it was a shattering blow, particularly at a time of high unemployment in the northwest and throughout Britain.

The takeover is somewhat ironic as in the early 1970s some in the betting shop industry feared the Tote would one day, through government legislation brought about by vociferous lobbying from the horse racing industry, take over all the UK's betting shops. The stance of the horse racing industry was to compare the system in the UK with countries where a state-sponsored pari-mutuel system was in force and to proclaim that betting shops were draining money away from racing and were thus the cause of all the sport's woes.

*

Returning to 1972, Grand Metropolitan also chose this year to finalise their long-term plan to take over the Ron Nagle chain of betting shops, a medium-size company based mainly in the Finsbury Park, Manor House and Tottenham areas of North London. The plan included the merger of the Ron Nagle group of shops with the already powerful Grand Metropolitan-owned City Tote chain and to put them all under the management of the Mecca Organisation to trade as Mecca Bookmakers Ltd.

Most of City Tote's directors and senior managers were let go, as the intention was for the the directors and senior management of the Ron Nagle group to run the whole show. I remained, and when I and the other branch managers met with Ron Nagle (chairman), Alan Nagle (chief executive) and Bob Green (development director) we came to understand how their coup had taken place during this merger. Just as with Con and Albert at Connor's, the Nagles and their senior management team were dyed-in-the-wool, old-school bookmakers. Their professionalism, entrepreneurship and street-wise shrewdness shone through; we could see exciting times ahead.

But the changes were unsettling for many of the remaining City Tote staff. They feared their employment terms and conditions would change and shop managers were especially concerned that the 10% of net profit scheme would cease. Sensing this unrest, some in the new company, along with others in the industry, placed an advert in *The Sporting Life* and called a meeting for all those worried about their working conditions.

In the betting world this type of unrest was unheard of. In previous times bookmaking had been a good industry in which to work and betting shop staff had been well paid. It had, at times, been quite a difficult industry to get into. But the takeover of small- and medium-sized groups of shops by larger organisations did cause anxiety.

Until then it had been something of a cottage industry, with the employees knowing their employers personally and often working alongside them. Now this was all changing, and it seemed to many staff that faceless directors and accountants were now in control.

The advert announcing the meeting read: 'Concerned about your future? Get the TUBE to Charing Cross'. It gave a date, time and place for the meeting and a brief synopsis of the items to be discussed. These included premium payments for Saturday and Bank Holiday working, payments when working short of staff, payments for the settler that were based on the number of betting slips taken and other issues that were generally talked of and griped about in the industry. The meeting was to be held in a room above a pub near Charing Cross. The advert explained that TUBE stood for The Union of Bookmakers' Employees.

Intrigued, I went along. The room was packed and I saw many City Tote staff there as well as other company shop managers and staff whom I knew, including rivals in the London Bookmakers' Darts League that had been formed by various betting office companies.

*

Somewhat surprisingly the chairman of the union meeting was Don Bruce, the owner of a chain of 12 betting shops in the Harrow area of northwest London. A committee was formed and the meeting started. As expected, most just wanted to have a moan about their salary and working conditions. There was a question from the floor, posed to Bruce, asking why, as an owner and employer, he had chosen to organise such a gathering. He replied that he simply wanted the betting industry staff to have good working conditions.

Some accepted this explanation, but cynics thought Bruce had an ulterior motive. No one could be sure, but he had a reputation as a good and fair man, and his employees enjoyed working for him.

It was agreed that the Union should go forward, and hold committee meetings to discuss future plans. During these subsequent meetings the possibility of strike action throughout the betting shop industry was seriously discussed. The committee also talked about approaching the print workers to see if *Sporting Life* would join the strike, or whether the supply of betting slips to the shops could be disrupted.

None of this strike talk came to anything. The union could not keep the momentum going, it attracted few subscription paying members and, although it tried hard to galvanise support, never really took off. In 1976 it fell under the banner of the Transport and General Workers Union (TGWU) and was rarely heard of again.

There was one noticeable exception when staff at a large Liverpool-based company, Stanley Racing, gained union recognition. This was only because, in the early 1980s, Stanley Racing had taken over a group of shops trading under the name Mercury Racing from whom the TGWU had previously gained union recognition. But in later years Stanley Racing was taken over by the William Hill organisation and union recognition ceased soon after as it could not get a majority of staff in the newly formed company to join the union.

Many years later, at the start of the 21st century, employees were again offered a betting shop-specific union under the name of Community. Otherwise, the industry has remained union free which is one of the reasons why such initiatives as opening shops in the evenings, Sundays and on Good Friday, wall-to-wall racing, constant availability of sports-betting opportunities, the introduction of gaming machines coupled with the extra responsibilities these have brought, have met with little resistance or protest from staff. Though it is important to remember that these initiatives have been the saviour for shops, and the reason why many jobs have remained.

Despite there being little union representation for staff, most betting shop operators do have some form of communication line between staff and directors. Many have a formal facility under set-ups such as staff councils in which employees can put their criticisms and comments directly to directors and senior executives.

*

Over the years, large multiples have bought up the majority of independent bookmakers. John Banks the flamboyant on-course bookmaker referred to earlier, had 34 betting shops in Scotland which he sold to Mecca in 1972 for a reported £1million. So much for his belief that betting shops were a 'licence to print money', or perhaps he felt the tide was turning.

The large multiples are mainly public limited companies or backed by private-equity institutions influenced by accountants. Their focus is the share price of the company and the rate of return on the investment. As with most businesses, staff costs are the largest controllable expense, so the wage bill and other staff benefits are under constant attack.

Latterly, one could not say that betting shop staff are overpaid but it remains a good source of employment for many who want to work in an industry where sport is key. And it offers good opportunities for promotion.

It is puzzling why trade unions were unable to get a strong foothold. It may be because betting shops are self-contained units, staffed by small groups who have little contact with fellow employees in other parts of the company or indeed other firms.

The bookmakers were themselves, until late 1973, all represented by a trade association known as the NAB (National Association of Bookmakers) and the NSL (National Sporting League). One of the directors of the NAB was Cyril Stein, at the time the leading light at Ladbrokes.

*

With the large companies such as the Mecca Organisation coming into the off-course (betting shop) industry, another trade organisation sprang into existence. BOLA, the Betting Office Licensees' Association, was specifically formed to protect the interests of betting shop owners. Its president was Lord Wigg and its chairman Eric Morley of Mecca Miss World fame. Representatives from William Hill, Ladbrokes, Coral and other major companies soon joined the board.

BOLA thus started off with big hitters and, even though it has now changed its name to the ABB (Association of British Bookmakers) it has continued to be a major influence in the betting industry that has lobbied and influenced many governments over the years.

Other betting trade associations still exist, notably the National Association of Bookmakers (NAB) and the Independent Bookmakers Association (IBA). NAB is focussed on betting in relation to horse and greyhound racing and how legislation affects both off-course and on-course bookmakers. The IBA, as its title suggests, is mostly concerned with the interests of the smaller independent bookmaker.

Nowadays, therefore, if any department in government, organisation or any part of the media wants to know what the views of the majority of betting shop operators, their first call is to the ABB which currently represents 85% of the UK's 8,500 betting shops.

Tom Kelly, a shrewd Scotsman, journalist and former editor of the *Sporting Chronicle* was chief executive of the ABB/BOLA for a long time. He managed to keep both large organisations and small independents on the same track, steering the industry safely through many a storm and was instrumental in introducing many of the innovations the modern-day betting shop offers. In a respectful and affectionate, but nevertheless humorous, vein he is sometimes referred to as Tombola.

Since Kelly's retirement from BOLA (ABB) in 2008, the organisation has been led by Russ Phillips, Andrew Lyman, Patrick Nixon and now Dirk Vennix, previously director of communications at the Tobacco Manufacturers' Association (TMA).

*

By early 1974 I had gained rapid promotion within the (now) Mecca Bookmakers organisation and worked as a relief area manager, covering for area managers when they were on holiday and assisting the regional director. My region spanned from King's Cross to the outskirts of Middlesex, and from Harrow to Kensington.

My last shop before this promotion was in Crouch Hill, North London, which took over 1,000 bets Monday to Friday and more than 3,500 each Saturday. On Saturdays extra staff were drafted in and the shop had seven cashiers taking bets and paying out winners.

We had three other settlers while I managed the shop and also settled bets. The shop also had settling machine, called a Bettie, but it was rarely used. Bettie was the size of a desk and, unlike today's settling machines, performed as if it was steam driven. It was much slower than either me or the other settlers in the branch.

In those days shops took far more bets across the counter than now, but even so Crouch Hill was exceptional. By 2.30pm on a Saturday afternoon when the pubs started to close it would be packed with men, fresh from drinking and keen to try to win some money.

Meanwhile, the miners were again threatening strike action and in February 1974, with the war between the Arab countries and Israel causing disruption to oil supplies, they did exactly that. In an attempt to conserve energy Prime Minister Edward Heath announced the three-day week. Factories, shops and offices were allowed to use electricity for only three days each week and only during certain times. There were heavy fines for organisations found to be using electricity outside these times – and these restrictions had a great effect on the betting industry.

Although some betting shops did close during the switch off, the more entrepreneurial operators managed to get around the problem. The senior managers at Mecca, myself included, were tasked to come up with a plan of how to keep the shops operational during the power cuts. A list of the essential equipment that would not work during the 'electricity off' period, was quickly identified and consisted in chief of the tills, race-broadcast amplifiers/speakers, security-microfilm cameras, lighting and heating.

We soon discovered we could operate the tills by cranking them with a handle. The race-broadcast amplifier and speakers could be powered by battery. The security-microfilm camera could be powered by emergency power units (EPUs) rigged up by Mecca's electronics department. EPUs were heavy-duty car batteries that could be charged up by the mains and then used to power the camera when there was no electricity. Mecca's bought hundreds of paraffin heaters for staff behind the counter and caravan-type gas lamps and candles were used to provide lighting. Mecca shops were ready and prepared for whatever was to come.

One wonders what modern health and safety executives would make of the naked flames of candles and gas lamps being in such close proximity to paraffin heaters! It all worked well though, apart from a shortage of gas canisters and mantles for the lamps.

The miners' strike ended after Ted Heath called a general election with the rallying cry: 'Who runs the country?' But he had misjudged the feelings of the nation, who although they had little sympathy for the miners, nevertheless longed for a return to normality. Consequently the Labour party was voted in, in the belief that they would be more sympathetic to the pay rises demanded by the miners and that normality would be restored.

Betting shop operators were now becoming sensitive to any threat to their turnover. Such events as transport strikes, power cuts, foot-and mouth-epidemics, newspaper strikes and bad weather were all scrutinised to see if there were ways to minimise disruption.

One initiative was the organisation of a constant programme of afternoon greyhound racing. The greyhound racecards were printed in *The Sporting Life* and the racing would be covered in full by Extel, with commentaries broadcast to shops should bad weather affect horse racing. An important side benefit of having the cards in *The Sporting Life* was that it put greyhound racing more centrally in the public domain and led people towards the sport. And of course punters could still place bets on these meetings whether horse racing was abandoned or not.

Almost all the greyhound tracks signed up, for a fee, to allow their results to be relayed to the betting shops. But some had second thoughts or wanted a higher fee for their racing and results and subsequently changed their minds. These were before the days of mobile phones and public phones were not available at greyhound stadiums.

How then to keep the public interested and betting on the afternoon's events, and get the results to the shops if Extel were not allowed to cover the greyhound racing programme? Ever entrepreneurial, the betting shop industry arranged for a representative to be at the appropriate stadium – Stamford Bridge was one such. Armed with eight tennis balls the representative would, after each race, cut open the rubber tennis ball, write the full result on a piece of paper, place it inside the tennis ball and throw it over the stadium wall. The catcher would use a nearby public telephone box to phone the results to a pre-arranged base, who would then quickly contact other bookmakers in the communication chain. These bookmakers would relay the results further down the line. It may sound directly out of a Monty Python sketch but, like so many simple systems, it worked.

Another initiative introduced in the summer of 1974, or perhaps I should say re-introduced, was betting on football. Bookmakers had all but stopped betting on football matches following the introduction of the 42% tax on stakes on fixed-odds football betting in 1972. But, always looking for an opening, the major bookmakers together with a Scottish bookmaker named John MacFarlane, trading under the 22-shop chain of Queen Bookmakers, forced the issue in law.

*

MacFarlane finally achieved a court ruling that determined the launch of the football coupon which contained individually priced matches where the odds could and would fluctuate (due to weight of money or other circumstances), and were only be subject to the current rate of betting duty – 7% of stakes. So whereas previously the bookmakers football coupon would advertise, for example '33-1 for three draws', now the coupon would have matches with individual odds marked against each team.

Most matches would advertise 2-1 or thereabouts for the draw and although a treble on three draws may return 33-1 for some matches it may return more. Also, the coupon would state words to the effect that 'these odds are subject to change'. Thus the 42% tax on fixed-odds football betting was avoided and instead the bets attracted only the 7% tax rate. Football betting was thus once more available to betting shop customers and its popularity, particularly in Scotland for some reason, was immediate. Certainly the industry is indebted to John MacFarlane, who died in 2006 at the great age of 96.

In the summer of 1974 as it was getting over the miners' strike, the betting shop industry was hit with another incident that caused headlines, the Gay Future coup. The August Bank Holiday of 1974 was chosen as the date for the coup, and Cartmel, a small remote course in Cumbria, as the place. Betting shops would be busy and Cartmel had no 'blower' system – the 'blower' being a direct phone link between the course and betting shop head offices.

Gay Future was a useful horse, brought over from Ireland by owner and Cork builder Tony Murphy and thereafter trained by Tony Collins. The plan was to keep Gay Future out of the way, train him to perfection but parade another lookalike horse, a real no-hoper, around Collins's yard and pass it off as Gay Future for the benefit of the public, any visitors or onlookers at the stable or training gallops.

On the day of the race, a group who became known as the 'Cork mafia' placed bets in shops all over London and elsewhere. They also planned to link the bets on Gay Future with bets on two other horses in doubles and trebles. These other two horses were called Opera Cloak and Ankerwyke. The perpetrators knew these other two horses would not run in the races they were entered for.

The gang linked bets on Gay Future with non runners in the knowledge that if relatively large single bets, say £50 each, were placed by strangers in betting shops solely on Gay Future (an infrequently run horse showing at 10-1 in the morning papers, at a meeting such as Cartmel) someone somewhere would realise something odd was going on.

*

Maybe a shop manager or someone in a head office would smell a rat, make a few phone calls to colleagues and the alarm bells would start ringing. But if the £50 stake was placed with two other horses in 3 x £10 doubles and a £20 treble, with the other two horses subsequently not running, there would be a bet of £40 going on to Gay Future (the other £10 being returned as a void double on the two non runners). In the main, win bets involving doubles and trebles do not cause much concern. Hence the doubles and trebles were successfully placed without any initial raised eyebrows.

To add to the plan, soap flakes were rubbed into Gay Future's legs to produce a lather when he was paraded prior to the race, in the hope that racegoers would believe the horse was sweating up, discouraging them from betting on him, thus keeping the odds at 10-1. The jockey also added a bit of flavour to the proceedings when he fell off the horse in the parade ring. So, the picture of a nervous horse ridden by an inexperienced rider was set for any onlookers. In fact the jockey was Timmy Jones, a more than capable rider from Ireland.

With the bets placed, the other two horses not running and most of the money bet riding on Gay Future, who started at 10-1, the coup was away. The horse romped home, winning by a distance, and the payout has been estimated at £1million (approximately five times that in today's money).

Unfortunately the Cork mafia had not counted on the jungle drums that beat in betting shops. When Gay Future won, their bets attracted the attention of shop managers – as did most large winning bets. Certainly a potential payout of £450 in 1974, to a stranger, or at least someone whose handwriting was not recognised would, or should, raise an eyebrow.

Shop managers are a talkative bunch and in constant phone contact with each other during the afternoon. If nothing else, they give each other moral support, discussing the last drunk they had to throw out, the last bet dispute they had, the quickest way to settle a bet, or in which pub the local managers would be meeting for a drink after work that night.

No doubt, during one of these phone calls, two managers discovered they had taken an unusual but identical bet. A phone call to head office would uncover the whole plot, as head office would then contact all the shops in their chain, and then the other betting shop organisations.

Eventually BOLA got involved and soon uncovered the complete picture; their investigations aided by a racing journalist who pounced on the story. When he telephoned the yard of Opera Cloak and

Ankerwyke, a stable girl innocently informed the journalist that, rather being on their way back from Plumpton and Southwell, where they had been due to race, or ill in their boxes, the two horses were happily grazing in a nearby field.

My involvement in this was to visit all the Mecca shops in the region to collect and collate all the relevant bets. I then delivered the bets to Mecca's head office in Finsbury Park where they were put with others collected from the other two regions in the company. The handwriting on the bets was compared and categorised and our findings were passed on to BOLA.

*

BOLA advised its members not to make payment on the bets, pending an enquiry. They also called for an investigation. The police got involved as the IRA was active at this time and there was a belief that they might be behind the coup. The main perpetrators, Murphy and Collins, were subsequently arrested and charged with attempted fraud.

The case was heard in Preston, where those in court believed the judge was rather sympathetic to the accused. After the jury brought in a guilty verdict – possibly partly due to anti-Irish feeling as the IRA bombing campaign was at its height – the judge was quoted as telling Murphy: 'It would be wrong to think of you as a fraudulent man and to send you to prison.' He described Collins as 'a man who has very fine qualities'. They were each fined £1,000 and were free to leave. To carry on the fallacy that these were, in some way, honest rogues, a film was made of the story – called Murphy's Stroke.

I thought the two got away lightly and that the judge sent out a message that they did little harm. Little sympathy had been shown to those punters who had bet on the form horses in the Gay Future race who lost their money because of the fraud. Moreover, it was an unfortunate signal to other fraudsters to try similar deeds.

Possibly just as famous as the Gay Future tale is the coup orchestrated by Barney Curley, a man whose name, over many years, has sent shivers down the spines of bookmakers. In June 1975, at Bellewstown racecourse near Dublin, he brought off a gamble that in today's money would be worth over £1.4million.

Curley's horse Yellow Sam, ran a number of races at other tracks in going conditions which did not suit him. Consequently, when Yellow Sam ran at Bellewstown he did so with considerably less weight than he should have. Bookmakers and punters at Bellewstown thought little of the horse's chances and he started at 20-1.

Just before the race, Curley organised for his agents to place sums of between £50 and £300 on the horse in off-course betting shops. At the same time he had another accomplice, Benny O'Hanlon, occupy the only public phone on the course. O'Hanlon was supposedly trying to get through to a hospital where his aunt was dying – a ploy that tied up the phone and stopped off-course bookmakers from getting money back to the course and shortening the price.

Not wanting to be seen at the course, Curley watched the race hidden in a gorse bush in the middle of the track and saw Yellow Sam win by two and a half lengths.

Although this book is about betting shops and not horse racing per se, it would be remiss if some horses and their achievements were not given a mention, not least because it was this sport which spawned the betting shop industry and all that followed – employment for tens of thousands and fortunes won and lost.

*

Everybody has their own favourite, but there is one horse whose name rings a bell with all: Red Rum. No horse before or since has won the Grand National three times. Red Rum won it in 1973, 74 and 77, was runner-up in 1975 and 1976. Some say that at least one of these runner-up placings might have been a win if different tactics had been employed.

I met Red Rum in the 1980s when, as an area manager, I thought it would be a good marketing ploy to invite him to the opening of a new shop in my area. That was in City Road, just a few yards from

Moorfields Eye Hospital. What a crowd Red Rum pulled and he certainly seemed to enjoy the attention – with his lad feeding him Polo mints all day long, the horse was in his element. This was the only day my daughter Lisa ever ventured into a betting shop. She has no interest in betting but she had heard of Red Rum and wanted to see him. I also got talking with another lady at the shop opening. She had heard that Red Rum would be at the event and had travelled from Newcastle just to see him. Red Rum: a crowd puller and pleaser indeed.

Other celebrities regularly carried out official openings of new or refurbished shops, including the likes of Derek Thompson, Frank Bruno, John Francome, Henry Cooper, Geoff Capes, John McCririck and *Sun* page three girls such as Linda Lusardi.

When Cooper opened one of my shops I did not have the courage to remind him of the Bugner fight and to tell how his defeat had earned me a large bonus that year.

*

Red Rum deservedly takes first place among my greats of horse racing but the first to capture the hearts of the public, back in the 1960s, was the outstanding three-time Cheltenham Gold Cup winner Arkle, who is still widely regarded as the greatest steeplechaser of all time.

Others who caught the headlines and the imagination during the 1970s were Nijinsky, the Triple Crown winner of 1970, and Mill Reef who won the Derby and Prix de l'Arc de Triomphe in 1971.

*

But back to greyhound racing and to Rochester greyhound stadium on 27 May 1978. A competition had been devised, open to greyhounds from other tracks, called the Long and Short Trip Stakes. Two heats would be run over 277 metres but the final, to be held on the same night, was to be run over 901 metres. Two greyhounds, Leysdown Pleasure and Leysdown Fun, ran in different heats and although they had good sprint form the bookmakers at the course offered unusually good odds for both in their first leg heats. Leysdown Pleasure started at 33-1 and Leysdown Fun at 4-1. Both won.

The picture above shows a group of my colleagues and Linda Lusardi at the opening of my refitted shop in Eastcheap. I am second from the right. Note the grass-effect carpet which was part of Mecca Bookmakers 'A day at the races' shop theme, at the time. The racing mural on the wall adds to the effect.

Geoff Capes, a true gentle giant, with me at the opening of a new shop in City Road. His fist is almost the same size as my head! I hope that doesn't say more about my head than his fist.

Frank Bruno did several shop openings for me. This one was in Ludgate Hill. Looking rather thin at this time, I was running regularly in preparation for the London Marathon.

Red Rum wins the Grand National for the second successive year in 1974.

The following morning, betting shop managers called their head offices to report that, unusually, single and double bets had been taken on these two greyhounds at Rochester, which was not a popular stadium with off-course punters.

Once again I was tasked to collate all Mecca's bets and deliver them safely to head office where they could be studied. A pattern started to emerge and other companies were contacted. BOLA was informed of the situation and advised its members to withhold payment, pending an enquiry.

The suspicion was that most bookmakers at the course had known what 'good things' the two greyhounds were. These bookmakers, despite the weight of money bet, had deliberately offered long prices on both, 'knocked them out' is the expression. The on-course bookmakers involved had, of course, placed substantial bets off course, in betting shops, on the winning pair. A judicial review found that the races had been 'deliberately framed to benefit a minority' and supported the betting shop operators' action in withholding payment on the bets. Estimates of the total potential payout ranged from £300,000 to £1million.

Similar to the Gay Future scam, in August 1978 there was another incident with a 'ringer' – one racehorse being substituted for another. A horse trained by John Bowles called In The Money won at Newton Abbott and, although there were no large or unusual bets reported, there were suspicions from some horse racing insiders that the horse was not In The Money but a rather better one in Cobblers March.

A police investigation followed and charges of conspiracy to defraud were brought against the trainer and jockey. Both pleaded not guilty. The jockey was acquitted but the trainer, Bowles, was found guilty and sentenced to 18 months' imprisonment suspended for two years. Following a Jockey Club hearing he was declared a disqualified person for 20 years.

On the face of it there was not much difference between Bowles's actions and those of the protagonists in the Gay Future coup, yet the subsequent punishment meted out was uneven to say the least.

On mornings following those coups in which bet payments were refused, managers would sometimes be unable to enter their shops – because the locks had been glued up. It was a way of trying to intimidate the shop owners into paying the bets in dispute. It was a warning that if the bets were not paid, more aggravation would come their way.

However, betting shop owners were, especially in these early days, shrewd guys. They knew that paying on a disputed bet because of intimidation would only encourage similar scams, so few, if any, paid up.

In any event the glue-ups, and other attempts at intimidation, were easily dealt with. Managers found that taking the precaution of spraying three-in-one oil into the locks as they left for the night stopped the glue from setting. They were also given a crash course in how to get into their own shops by taking off the beading that held the glazing in place on the front door. If the lock was a Yale-type, the front door could usually be opened from the inside.

*

The 1970s cannot be left behind without mentioning two characters who were famous in their own right, but who also had an ongoing public feud. Remember John Banks, the Scottish bookmaker who stood his ground against the off-course betting shop operators who sent money back to the course in an effort to shorten the price of a selection. If Banks thought a favourite, or any other fancied horse, could be beaten he would not cut the price but instead lay bets all day, despite the efforts and weight of money from companies such as Ladbrokes. Cyril Stein had founded Ladbrokes and was unlikely to take kindly to a relatively small bookmaker standing in the way of Ladbrokes' plans to shorten the price of a horse. No doubt other off-course bookmakers were also not pleased at the Banks' antics.

What the off-course betting shop operators were doing was quite acceptable. They were simply sending money back to the course, if they recognised that the weight of money they had taken in their shops did not equate with the odds offered by the on-course bookmakers. What Banks was doing was a glorified type of punting. He was using his own view of a horse's form to make a book, rather than the accepted way of using weight of money to determine a horse's odds.

This bear trading must have over-spilled into something personal as Banks tried to name one of his own racehorses Greenwich Mean Stein. Weatherbys blocked the use of the name so on a somewhat sarcastic note, Banks named the horse Adorable Cyril.

Banks courted controversy and publicity and two of his notable actions were the purchases of Hill House and later in 1974 the coup horse Gay Future. Hill House surprisingly won the Schweppes Gold Trophy by 12 lengths in 1967 but was found at a subsequent dope test to have abnormal amounts of cortisol in his system. His trainer, Captain Ryan Price, put forward the explanation that the horse had probably produced its own cortisol during the running and excitement of the race. Veterinary tests showed the horse could indeed have produced the drug.

However, Hill House, although running several more times in Banks' colours, never won another race. Banks said that after each race he had Hill House tested and no trace of cortisol was ever found.

A defining incident for Banks came in 1978 when a horse called Stopped, ridden by John Francome, was 9-4 favourite for the Imperial Cup at Sandown and finished third. After a stewards' inquiry, Francome was cautioned for riding an 'ill-judged' race. It was subsequently learnt that Francome and Banks had been in regular contact, although Banks denied he had profited from information about Stopped's form or that he ever gave favours in return for information from the jockey.

After the Jockey Club inquiry, Banks and Francome were found guilty of 'conduct likely to cause serious damage to the interests of horse racing'. The counsel for the Jockey Club, however, stressed that dishonest 'stopping' of horses was not alleged.

Banks failed to overturn the decision in the High Court and was warned off racecourses for three years and fined £2,500; Francome was fined £750 and suspended for the remainder of that season. Banks returned to the racecourse following his suspension but had lost his appetite for publicity. He had, for well over a decade, been a charismatic character in the betting industry, and died in August 2003 at the age of 68.

Given their open hostility towards each other, Cyril Stein may have enjoyed Banks' punishment, but he was to have his own highly embarrassing and expensive moment only a few years later.

Ladbrokes' casino division had a 27% market share in 1979 but Stein wanted more. Thus a high-ranking marketing executive in the division hatched a plan to attract more high rollers to their casinos. The initiative, codenamed Unit Six, determined to find out which big spenders were using other casinos and then entice them to use the Ladbrokes casinos. The number plates of cars parked outside casinos were noted and then, quite illegally, the car owners' names and addresses were obtained. Champagne and other luxury items was then

William Hill with his horses Ballymoss and Celtic Ash.

sent with an invitation encouraging them to use the Ladbrokes casinos.

Private Eye exposed the ploy and the police objected to the renewal of Ladbrokes' casino licences. Stein adamantly denied that he or any of Ladbrokes' senior management knew of the scheme. But his involvement was fatally exposed when his personal secretary, Janet Ballard, went into the witness box. A churchgoing middle-aged lady, Ballard told the court that one morning Stein had come to work at 8.30am and ordered her to shred all the files relating to the Unit Six project.

The judges took just 10 minutes to take away the licences and the casinos were permanently closed that afternoon. It was estimated the company lost in excess of £100million as a result. Perhaps Banks had a wry smile on his face when he read the reports of the hearing.

It is probably appropriate to conclude my memories of the 1970s with those of another character with a similarly exuberant style to Prince Monolulu. John McCririck, an investigative journalist with *The Sporting Life*, burst on to the scene in 1978 when he won the Specialist Writer of the Year in the British Press Awards. In 1979 he was named Campaigning Journalist of the Year.

McCririck made his name with a story that uncovered how some were able to place bets on greyhounds that had already won. He discovered and reported how Extel broadcast the off-times for greyhound races to betting shops only to the nearest minute and were occasionally slow in picking up the commentary from the course. In doing so, they enabled astute punters who had accomplices at the course, to place late bets in the shops.

Then, in 1979, he exposed a story that was to become known as 'Totegate'. With the agreement of senior executives at the Tote, employees were putting winning bets placed off-course into the Tote pool after the result was known. It was all done in an effort to suppress winning bet dividends and thereby increase profits for the Tote.

*

Since then McCririck, due to his knowledge, outspokenness and

John McCririck.

manner of dress, has developed a long career in television. He is also much in demand by betting shop owners as a celebrity guest who will always draw a large crowd at the opening of a new shop.

On one of many occasions when Mecca employed him to open a new shop, a large crowd arrived early at the shop in the Stamford Hill area of London, waiting to see McCririck. He duly arrived wearing his trademark deerstalker hat and cape, smoking a large cigar and with the 'Booby', his wife, in tow. He thrilled the crowd with his comments and stories and tipped them the winner of the first race. He stayed at the shop for as long as was needed, until the last autograph hunter was satisfied, then he was off, job well done.

Love him or loath him, the industry needs characters and should cherish any such as Big Mac.

CHAPTER SIX

THE 1980S

Shergar, Terry Ramsden, What Makes a Profitable Betting Shop, Customer Service, Bob Green, Live Racing Pictures, SIS, Licence Applications, Lester Piggott Goes To Jail, *Racing Post*, Staff Issues, High Rollers and Betting Tax,

By the start of the 1980s, the directors and senior executives at Mecca Bookmakers considered that I had earned my stripes and after a management restructure I was appointed area manager of what was known within Mecca as the City area. This covered the shops located east to Whitechapel, west to Holborn, north to King's Cross and south to the Thames. The patch had a good mix of shops, staff and issues, but most importantly it contained shops in and around the prestigious financial hub that is the City of London.

For the previous few years I had been auditing shops, helping with promotions and marketing, searching for and recommending new licence applications, keeping an eye on the activity of competitors, assisting other area managers in investigating internal staff fraud and external customer fraud, organising and conducting manager training sessions and a host of other interesting tasks. There were now around 13,250 betting shops and Mecca Bookmakers was a major player in the industry.

Now I had my own shops, staff and administration team to work with and develop. The UK was just coming out of a recession and the City, with its financial institutions, retail shops, bars and restaurants was vibrant. This feel-good factor was mirrored throughout the rest of the country.

Being an area manager had its benefits. One was training and developing shop staff to reach their full potential. Although Mecca had a regional personnel department that had the main responsibility for finding staff, recruitment was also a part of my remit. This enabled me to help any able family members looking for permanent, temporary or casual employment, but I would only ever engage those that were up to the job.

One such time was when my brother-in-law Paul was attending medical school and was looking for work during the university summer break. I arranged for him to have a job as a temporary boardman. Paul now has a masters from Harvard and is a senior hospital consultant specialising in thoracic medicine, but he often refers to those boardman days.

*

The board was in the customer area of the shop where Paul worked, and enabled him to overhear the punters' crazy conversations. These would often consist of unfounded stories relating to jockeys taking bribes, trainers having magical powers, bookmakers being crooks, mad betting systems that were supposedly successful and a host of other illogical theories. Paul says being a boardman was the best job he ever had. For those who have experienced it, the job and the characters one meets in the industry get into the blood and stay with you.

It would be interesting to learn how many high-flyers and famous folk were once employed in betting shops. It seems to attract a certain type of character and is a big magnet for university students who are looking for summer vacation work. With regular staff on holiday a raft of replacements is needed during the summer months when many betting shops are at their busiest.

I know myself that many teachers, doctors, nurses, scientists, actors, authors, journalists and the like have been employed in the industry. I have no doubt that the experience of dealing with the betting public will have helped to develop their character and stood them in good stead in their future lives and careers. I know that John McCririck has done his stint on a betting shop board and has tried his hand as a settler. I also know of at least one senior journalist at the *Racing Post* who has done a stint behind the counter and as a boardman.

*

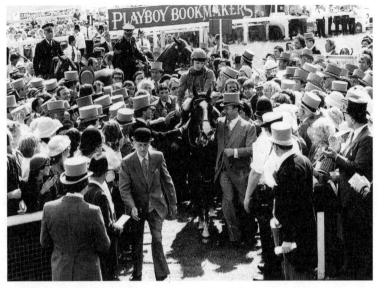

Shergar, winner of the 1981 Derby.

In 1981, Shergar captured the public's imagination when, with his tongue lolling out of one side of his mouth, a white blaze on his face and white markings on his shins, he won the Derby by a record-breaking 10 lengths.

Fast forward less than two years to February 1983 and the nation was shocked and gripped with sadness, when it learnt that Shergar had been stolen from his stables at the Ballymany Stud, County Kildare, Ireland and a ransom of £2million demanded. Many wild theories began as to who had carried out the kidnapping, with suggestions as diverse as the Mafia and Colonel Gaddafi of Libya.

Some members of the IRA have since admitted to taking part in the kidnap and killing the stallion soon after he was abducted. There was always little chance that their ransom request would yield the required £2million as Shergar was owned by a syndicate rather than a single owner. Reaching agreement between all the parties was

111

unlikely and yielding to the demands would have opened the door to copycat crimes. Nevertheless, Shergar will be remembered as a brilliant racehorse who met a terrible end but touched the hearts of all those who knew of him.

*

I relished developing my area and enjoyed the managerial responsibilities. My group of shops constantly performed above expectations. Monetary and bet-slip turnover had increased, net profit was always above expectations and expenses were kept tightly under control. In fact, throughout the 1980s, business throughout the Mecca estate was booming.

A prime example of the boom years of the 1980s were the antics of Terry Ramsden, whom I came across quite often as he was based in the City and used many of the Mecca (and Ladbrokes) shops in the vicinity.

Although there were a number of high rollers betting in my area, Ramsden, who mainly frequented shops around Moorgate and City Road, beat them all. He, or his runners, would think nothing of walking into a shop, opening up a case full of money and proceeding to place large stake bets such as £1,000 yankees with a total stake of £11,000, or £25,000 to win. This happened not just once but several times a day and most days of the week, and if they lost, they wouldn't bat an eyelid.

When Ramsden first started his bets were treated with caution and suspicion that he was getting inside information. Over time, however, it became clear that his bets were, more often than not, losers – indeed many of his selections never even had a mention from the commentator.

These were still the days when Mecca managers were on commission if their shops earned a net profit. And, to top it all, my staff found Ramsden to be a charming and patient person who was easy to deal with. In more ways than one he was the ideal customer.

*

All good things come to an end, however, and in 1987 Ramsden's company Glen International collapsed. He had also been betting on credit with other major bookmakers and losing vast sums. It was rumoured that when Glen International collapsed Ramsden, who had been placing bets sometimes to a value of £1million, had lost £58million to Ladbrokes.

Looking back, the Ramsden era seems surreal, especially when contrasted with the real world on my side of the betting shop divide in which, just as with any properly run organisation, business plans and budgets had to be set, staff employed, trained and motivated, projections made and every aspect of the business managed and monitored.

Betting shops, if managed properly, could be profitable. But in general they were no longer a licence to print money. Contrary to public belief, punters do have winning bets and they do get paid out. And as with any other business there is rent, rates and salaries to be paid plus repayments on any bank loans used to start the company.

One should think of bookmaking, or running a betting shop, as similar to that of running an insurance company. Premiums are received which are used to meet the claims made and paid on policies. Sometimes, however, an independent betting shop owner with maybe two or three shops can strike it lucky and attract the custom of a one-off high roller. The decision then would be whether to stand all or some of the bet, or find a bookmaker who would pay a small commission for the bet to be passed on to him.

It is no good finding premises where the turnover is expected to be good if the rent and rates are exorbitant. Likewise, it is no good finding premises with low rent and rates if it is tucked away in a back street, far from a pub or factory and so with no prospect of adequate turnover. In a similar vein, having a high turnover and attracting business is no good if it is at the cost of giving prices, odds, bonuses or concessions that are out of kilter with the industry and are unprofitable. By the mid 1980s some operators were finding the going tough and due to rationalisation the number of betting shops had reduced to around 10,000.

I learnt all these basics at an early stage, but now I, and others at Mecca, were learning about staff motivation, business accountancy and staff-management techniques. The instigator for this was the chief executive at Mecca Bookmakers, Bob Green.

Bob introduced many initiatives to Mecca and to the industry in general. He ensured that his senior team were always kept up to speed with latest management techniques, relevant legislation, employment law, best practice as preached by the Industrial Society, betting politics and other aspects that would affect the business. The management team was constantly kept in the information loop and this developed a great team spirit.

*

The ethic was to work hard and play hard and the occasional Mecca promotional event served as a great diversion to the hands-on 24/7 work culture. Being part of the Mecca organisation meant receiving the occasional invitation to the glamorous Miss World competition and subsequent celebration ball, held respectively at the Royal Albert Hall and the Grosvenor House Hotel.

There was the chance to take trips on the liner QEII, on which Mecca had a casino, plus invitations to race meetings at York, where Mecca sponsored the Dante Stakes, and Sandown where they sponsored a major handicap hurdle and handicap chase. There were also occasional invites to racing at Ascot and Epsom where Mecca had boxes.

The Mecca box at Ascot was spectacular. Never wishing to be thought of as conventional, Bob Green had tasked his designers to come up with something different for the interior decoration. They came up with the theme of a Bedouin tent so striking that it caused neighbouring box holders to come and admire what had been achieved.

It was a similar story whenever a new shop design left the drawing board. Bob ensured that his designers came up with original themes for the interior and in the mid 1980s one design that had the opposition talking was the Mecca 'Day at the Races' concept.

In an effort to emulate what racegoers would see at the racecourse, in front of a bank of television screens would be a 'grandstand' of tiered, comfortable seating. Nearby would be a real tree, about three or four metres high, usually a fig tree as these were most likely to survive indoors. There would be air conditioning, refreshments near to hand and the floor covering would be either a grass-green carpet or a laminate floor with a grass-effect surface.

Corporate days were enjoyable, but their main purpose was to develop the team-building ethos and motivational strategy that Bob Green lived by. It certainly worked for his hardworking and loyal team.

In the late 1980s Bob took over as chairman of William Hill when Mecca and William Hill merged. John Brown, who was let go from Hill's when Bob took over, later asked in his book *Lucky John*, why if Mecca had the best management team as Bob Green claimed, did he say that William Hill had the best brand and why did he allow the merged company to be called William Hill?

With the greatest respect to John Brown, who is recognised as another giant of the betting industry, I should have thought the answer was obvious. And maybe, being a little biased, I shared Bob's belief when he said that Mecca Bookmakers had the best management team.

There were, however, some exceptions and as I met up and got to know some of the William Hill people it would be right to say that each company had its management strengths and weaknesses.

But, the reason Bob chose the name of William Hill for the newly merged set of companies was that Mecca had been trading for only a few years under that title as it was an amalgamation of several smaller operators, whereas William Hill was possibly the most famous name in bookmaking. The William Hill group of shops had been on the high street for almost 25 years.

*

William Hill was formed as a company in 1934 and thereafter Hill or his representative stood on their on-course pitch at most, if not all, horse race meetings. Hence the brand name was established on- and off-course. Being represented on the racecourse was something Mecca had not previously sought. The decision for the merged companies to trade as William Hill, although sad for the Mecca management team, was a no-brainer.

What Bob considered was that having the best-known brand did not automatically mean that the company had the best management team. Bob was particularly concerned with the importance of customer service in an era when punters were often still treated as 'the enemy'.

The prevalent attitude among betting shop operators was 'give the punters nothing, settle every bet strictly to the operating rules, even if we make a mistake make no gesture of goodwill and use no discretion'.

Bob, ever the innovator and entrepreneur, recognised that customers should be treated better, and saw this as a gap in the market. He consequently presented his Mecca Bookmakers Customers Come First campaign to his executives and senior managers one memorable evening at the Grosvenor House Hotel, Park Lane, in the spring of 1985.

Following this was a massive media, billboard, train and bus poster campaign which were his brainchild and which advertised the fact that Mecca, at least, placed customer service high on the agenda.

I remember two slides that Bob displayed at the Park Lane evening. His first slide showed the company structure as it was perceived by those within the operational side of the company, and one that all present recognised as the slippery career pole that they were attempting to climb:

Cashier

Shop manager

District manager

Area manager

Regional director

Operations director

Board

Bob then displayed a second slide which, he said, was the one those present should have as their mindset:

Customers
Cashier
Shop manager
District manager
Area manager
Regional director
Operations director
Board

Turning things on their head made quite a difference and it was certainly a notion that had most of those in the room, including myself, thinking differently.

It was therefore no surprise when, a year or so after introducing the customer service initiative, one of Mecca's manager's was named the inaugural *Racing Post* Manager of the Year.

Mecca's top manager, Willie Allinson (right), receives the "Betting Shop Manager of the Year" award from Brough Scott, Racing Post's *editorial director.*

Not long after the launch of the Customer Comes First campaign, Bob announced another initiative – believing the legislation by which betting shops were controlled was soon to be liberalised. Part of this liberalisation would be to allow television pictures to be broadcast live into betting shops.

*

Bob announced that, with the blessing of BOLA and for the benefit of the betting shop industry, he and his technology expert Bill Hogwood had formed a company called Satellite Racing Development (SRD). The objective was for SRD to research and put in place relevant technology, satellite facilities, mobile broadcasting vans, agreement from the racecourses and all the other ancillary, equally vital components to bring the vision of live racing broadcasts in betting shops to reality.

The 1986 Betting Shop Show advertised to all that live pictures in betting shops would indeed be a reality. Bob had organised a mock-up betting shop showing his vision for the future. The shop was carpeted, air-conditioned and fitted out in banquet-style leather sofas and chairs. There was a pizza cafe bar in one corner, a soft drinks, tea and coffee bar in another, a row of self-service bet-placement machines in another and, the pièce de résistance, a large screen projector covered one wall of the shop. This screen was showing live pictures and commentary from the main race meeting of the day.

Most of the major betting shop operators took shares in the new company. It was renamed Satellite Information Services (SIS) and almost every betting shop owner in the UK subscribed, putting the final nail into the coffin of the Extel audio-only broadcast service to betting shops.

In 1987, SIS prepared for its first broadcast – set for 5 May. Betting shops in Bristol were the first to receive the service, which was soon rolled out to the rest of the 10,400 betting shops in the UK and Ireland. What a success story. SIS now employs around 500 staff, has a turnover in excess of £200million and net profit in excess of £23million.

Where is Bob today? He is now based in America, still no doubt

Bob Green (to the top right of the picture) announces the successful progress of the satellite broadcasting initiative to a group of invited guests at the Mecca Bookmakers Hurdle at Sandown in 1986. My wife and I are somewhere in the far left corner. The mock satellites in the ceiling set the scene and the poster behind Bob proclaims to all: 'Satellite TV Racing, We (Mecca Bookmakers) Led The Way'.

introducing fresh initiatives to his Philadelphia Park horse racing track, on course-casino and associated off-course, high-specification betting premises, known as Turf Clubs.

The 1980s were exciting, vibrant times for betting shops. Ladbrokes, William Hill, Mecca, Coral, even the government-owned Tote were all expanding. Aside from the Tote, which had a remit to plough money back into horse racing, all the others were wondering how to best spend the cash reserves sitting on their balance sheets.

As an example, Ladbrokes were buying shops at a rate of knots at often premium prices. Cyril Stein, having recovered from the casino fiasco, seemingly did not have to answer to many other shareholders or investors when he considered buying a business. Ladbrokes were branching out and putting themselves into the headlines. They sponsored the University Boat Race and had saved the Grand National from possible extinction by managing it. In the late 1980s they also bought the Texas DIY business and Vernons Pools.

Once a suitable premises was found, to open a betting shop before 1988 required planning permission for a change of the use to a Licensed Betting Office. Dependent upon the local council this could be a stumbling block, although usually not an insurmountable one. Later, the New-Use Classes Order of 1988 declared that no planning permission was required if the premises for a new Licensed Betting Office had previously traded as a bank, building society, employment agency, estate agent, travel agent or similar.

It may all sound too easy to acquire a profitable betting shop and often it did seem to be, especially in the early years of live horse racing satellite broadcasts in betting shops.

*

Other areas that required attention were staff recruitment and discipline, and customer and staff fraud. One situation that sticks in my mind was when the regional personnel manager came into my office one day and told me he had just interviewed a man for a vacant trainee manager's job. The very experienced personnel manager was perplexed that the applicant, in his middle thirties, was a former Roman Catholic priest.

The personnel manager, knowing I was a Catholic, wanted a second opinion. I spoke to the ex-priest who explained that he had fallen in love with one of his parishioners and wanted to get married and start a family. He said finding employment after leaving the priesthood was not easy, but that he had always enjoyed horse racing and sports and thought he would try the betting industry.

The ex-priest produced his medal of office and relevant correspondence from the bishop, and he so oozed goodness and integrity that I did not hesitate to recommend that he be employed. He was taken on and, after training, I found a shop in my area for him to manage. Over time he developed into an able manager and excellent employee but sadly his 'love' changed her mind and decided not to marry him.

Another incident in which religion played a part was with a manager of a shop whose slip numbers were declining. I decided to pay the shop a visit and when I went behind the counter saw several posters on the wall of religious texts and images. Straight away the manager started to talk to me about Jesus and how he had found God. I could not help but reply that I did not know He was lost. It soon became obvious that the manager had been trying to enforce his religious views on the customers who had voted with their feet and gone elsewhere.

The manager then wanted to confess how, in the past, he had put through a few inflated petty-cash receipts for the purchase of newspapers. He explained he had done this to cover till discrepancies, probably caused by overpayments to customers. The total involved amounted to only a few pounds. I felt that I now had something of a quandary. False accounting within the company always resulted in instant dismissal but here was a manager who was totally upfront and, apart from possibly easing his conscience, had brought up something he had no need to declare. In essence the incident was minor but on the other hand it seemed that he was losing customers because of his zealous views on religion.

Fortunately, the dilemma resolved itself. The manager offered his resignation during our conversation, saying he did not feel that the bookmaking business was a morally correct one with which to be involved. I told the manager there was no need for him to work his notice period and that he could leave the branch immediately. With a 'may peace and God be with you' goodbye, he was off, problem solved.

Location, as with house buying, is the key to a good betting shop but the competence and motivation of the staff, in particular the manager, is pivotal. A good manager cannot only keep existing business but can also attract and encourage new trade, thus increasing profit. Employ, and do nothing about, a bad 'un and, soon, trade and profit will be lost.

*

Bad managers come in various guises. They can be bad timekeepers, either opening the shop late or closing it early. They can be bad attendees, going sick at the drop of a hat or just thinking that the annual sick leave is there to be used, whether they are genuinely ill or not. They may lack skill in customer care, be shaky on knowledge of the betting shop product or have poor motivational skill with their staff. The final but most unforgivable trait in this cash-generative business is that of dishonesty.

My administration team at the area office had, among other responsibilities, the duty of auditing the business from the shops in the area. This auditing included viewing the microfilm from the camera installed in the shops. Not every bet, from every day, from every shop, could be viewed, as this would take an army of staff to accomplish. So it was an open secret among betting shop staff that the microfilm check on bets for their shop was periodical. Managers also had to provide details of bets paid that came to over £100. So the assumption – an accurate one – was that bets with returns over £100 were checked as a matter of course.

But the periodical checks were not haphazard. There was a method for deciding which shops were to be looked at. In general this decision was based on a shop's recent gross profit (compared to the area average), turnover (money and slips) trend, and whether or not the manager was long-serving or a newcomer. Gut feeling, following a shop visit by my assistant area manager or myself, also played its part.

It was after a visit to a high-turnover shop with a long-serving manager near Fleet Street that I decided to follow up with an in-depth audit. During the visit the normally reserved manager could not wait to show me his figures for the past few months and described how well the shop was doing, both in turnover and profit. And indeed this was true, with a particularly good Derby day the previous week.

But, to me, the manager's overenthusiasm was out of character. Further checks confirmed that some winning bets had not been put through the microfilm. There were three in total, all placed on Derby day. The stakes on each of the bets (doubles and trebles) were all less than £10 but the returns on each were for sums in the region of £90. Remember that this was the mid 1980s and £250 cash in your pocket was a tidy sum.

After I had interviewed the staff, the manager was dismissed for gross misconduct and the matter reported to the police. He was charged and subsequently found guilty of fraud. In essence, the manager had believed that his length of service, reputation and good trading figures would ensure his shop was not checked on one of its busiest days of the year. He had registered three blank betting slips in one of the tills, had not processed them through the microfilm camera and, after the results were known, had written winners on to the slips. He had gambled and lost.

*

Other managers and staff suffer at the hands of fraudulent punters who coerce staff into colluding with them. A check on one shop that had been producing a less-than-average gross win percentage, showed that a punter had, for several weeks, been able to place bets after the off on greyhound races. In these races it appeared that the processing of the off-slip had been slightly delayed on one of the tills. It is common industry knowledge that the greyhound leading at the first bend has a better than 65% chance of winning the race.

Again, the staff were interviewed and the cashier was found to be acting in collusion with a punter in the placing of late bets, thus giving the punter a clear advantage. The punter had sweet-talked the female cashier into delaying the striking of the off-slips and taking his bets. The manager, who had taken it upon himself to settle bets in a back room, away from the counter, and thought the punter was just having a run of good luck. I was speechless at his naivety.

I concluded that both the cashier and manager should be dismissed; the cashier for gross misconduct and the manager for incompetence. The matter was also reported to police in the hope that the punter and cashier could be charged with conspiracy to commit fraud, gain pecuniary advantage or similar. But the local CID declined to become involved, citing that due to, in their opinion, lack of sufficient evidence it would not be in the public interest to pursue the matter.

This case had a sequel in that the manager took the company to an industrial tribunal, citing unfair dismissal. Not that I was in the habit of having staff dismissed unfairly, but I was no stranger to such courts. Part of the reason for this was that staff could take an action of unfair dismissal against a former employer at no cost. So, on the basis that there is nothing to lose, quite a few staff who were dismissed for various reasons chose to bring such a case against the company.

Due to ego, pride or a false sense of injustice, staff often cannot accept that they have acted in error. Unfortunately, in a betting shop, errors can cost a great deal of money. Although some are unavoidable, errors that could easily have been avoided are difficult to ignore or forgive.

In this case the manager's father, who probably had delusions about his son's ability, and who fancied himself as something of a lawyer, probably encouraged the action and represented him at the hearing. But when the evidence was laid in front of the court concerning the bets, the cost to the company, the disregard for normal shop procedures and a manager's duty regarding 'off slips', and the actions, or lack of them, of the manager one could see that the wind had been taken out of the father's sails. One wonders what tale his son had spun him about the whole matter.

Then another body blow: the father's main thrust to the court was that the microfilm camera clock was faulty and unreliable. This presupposed that the bets were therefore genuine and placed in time. But, ignoring this point for the moment, the main brick in his argument was that there was a period of time during the taking of the fraudulent bets when the camera clock showed some of the bets had been captured an hour before the off of the race; either that or the camera clock was running an hour slow.

*

One must remember that cases of this nature take many months to get to court. Also, the evidence asked for by the other party would be supplied as and when asked for. Again, this would be many months after the incident. So included in the bundle of evidence were printouts from the microfilm showing the bet and camera clock. Alongside this was a separate schedule showing the off and result times of the races in question. And yes, some of the bets did appear to be taken an hour before the race.

I was asked in the witness box how I could be so sure that the bets were late, bearing in mind the only evidence was a camera clock that showed some of the bets had been taken well in time. I explained to the court that some of the bets from the month of March were photographed in Greenwich Mean Time (GMT) whereas, at the time, the country was using British Summer Time (BST). I went on, the cameras were serviced by visiting engineers every three weeks or so and therefore when the clocks throughout the country went forward an hour (in March) to BST, the clocks installed in the microfilm cameras would still be set at GMT – showing an hour behind BST.

I concluded that when bets were viewed on the microfilm for this period of time, one simply had to add an hour to the time shown on the clock in the camera to get an accurate reading. It was not the case that the clock in the camera was faulty, or had lost an hour. It was simply that it had not been adjusted for BST.

The manager's father had no response. He had, surprisingly, not considered the change from GMT to BST. He had apparently jumped on what he thought was a weakness in the case that had been used to dismiss his son, the manager. The verdict went the company's way and the accusation of unfair dismissal was rejected.

After the case a young reporter approached me for a quote. This was the first time that I met Jim Cremin, stalwart of the *Racing Post* who reports on the betting shop scene. Jim had joined the paper a short time earlier after being employed as racing manager at Wembley greyhound stadium. He joined the *Racing Post* as a greyhound journalist but soon took on the additional mantle of covering betting shop matters. He has now been doing this job admirably for 25 years.

The quote I gave to Jim was the standard bland comment: 'We are pleased and were always confident the employment tribunal would reach the correct decision'. I overheard the quote the father was giving to Jim. It went something like: 'We are obviously disappointed and are considering appealing'. There was never an appeal.

But sometimes I did not get it right and learnt to my cost that managers could be their own worst enemies. One case involved a 19-year-old who had joined as a cashier, and was highly regarded by all the managers with whom he had worked. He applied and was accepted on the trainee manager's course which he duly passed and was allocated to a low-turnover shop. Early in the afternoon on his second day I took a phone call from the head office raceroom advising me that there seemed to be a large-staking punter at the branch this young chap was managing. The raceroom manager went on to relay several bets, ranging from £500 upwards, that had been notified to the raceroom, all of which were losers and so far they totalled £5,000.

*

I decided to visit the shop. When I got there, I found the manager had sent the cashier home as she had been feeling unwell. In the customer area there were two punters who were betting in £1s and £2s. I asked where the large-staking punter was and the manager stuttered an incoherent response. I asked to see where the £5,000 cash was that the punter had lost. The manager then admitted that there was no punter and that the bets were his. There was no cash as he had been placing the bets on credit, hoping to find a winner. The total that he now owed the till was £10,000 having bet on eight straight losers. Another instant dismissal ensued, followed by an application to Customs and Excise to be excused the tax due on the £10,000 registered on the till.

This type of incident is, sadly, not unusual. Though not a criminal offence, betting with the company in which you are employed is an offence punishable with dismissal. However, a manager placing a bet without the means to pay for it is a different matter. Desperation, boredom, the possibility of apparent easy pickings, a belief that 'this one can't get beat', are all reasons why a manager starts to bet in the shop. The betting almost always turns into betting on credit, with the bets getting bigger and bigger until that elusive winner is found or until the charade is uncovered.

Just as betting shop managers can be their own worst enemies, punters can also be the cause of a manager's downfall. Those in charge have to be on their guard at all times; one moment of weakness and someone will take advantage. There are too many such occasions to describe every one but the following are typical.

A regular customer, who bets race by race most days for sums of £25 or £40, puts a £40 bet on just before the off of a sprint race. He fumbles through his pockets and declares he can't find his money but will pay for the bet in a while. Instead of the cashier or manager taking immediate action and voiding the bet that had been registered through the till, a state of suspended reality takes place where no action is taken, as the manager looks at the cashier, who looks at the punter, who looks at the TV screens and the race is off. The bet is not recorded as void and passed through the microfilm camera, and thus remains live. The bet loses, the punter shrugs his shoulders.

Next he writes out a bet for £75 and offers it with no money. What should the manager do? If he refuses to take the bet the punter will become annoyed and leave the shop, not paying for the losing £40 bet. If the manager allows the bet to be taken and it loses, the punter then owes the shop £115 and the punter also has the manager committed to maybe taking further bets on credit.

How are these instances resolved? Either the punter eventually has a winner and the manager, with no doubt a huge sigh of relief, is able to balance the till using the winning betting slip. Or the punter runs up such a large debt that the manager has no option but to declare the same to his area manager/head office. Unfortunately for the manager and staff involved dismissal often follows. Very rarely does the punter simply get the money and settle the debt.

A ruse that some high-rollers attempt, and unfortunately one which still catches out betting shop staff, is 'the case full of money con'. Large-staking punters are almost invariably something of a headache, and often turn into a nightmare. They expect special treatment, want a back price or best price, have little patience and expect staff to take their large bets immediately, giving little or no time for the cash to be checked and the bet to be authorised by head office. Seldom are such high-rollers long-term customers, and will either disappear never to be seen again, or reduce their stakes to £1s, or try a last throw of the dice and attempt to con the shop staff.

Often these customers carry their cash in a briefcase that they hand to the staff saying the key is lost or combination temporarily forgotten. Staff will then stupidly allow bets to be laid on the strength that there is a large sum of cash in the case, as there had been on previous days. Sweet-talking and tips given on previous occasions by a high-roller often causes the staff to lower their guard. You do not need me to tell you what the outcome is when the bets are losers and the case is opened as the punter legs it out of the door.

Some punters not only act dishonestly but also in a rather inhumane way with no thought for others. On one occasion a pregnant cashier suddenly became ill in the shop. The only other member of staff was the manager and, while he was trying to take care of the cashier he was momentarily unable to take all of the bets that were being offered. Rather than show sympathy to the plight of the staff, most of the customers proceeded to abuse and threaten the manager for not taking the bets.

This was not an isolated incident and many similar stories could be told. Worst of all was when a customer suffered a heart attack as he was placing a bet. The two staff on duty rushed to his aid only for other customers to gain access to the unattended staff area and steal the cash available. Others complained that their bets were not being taken. All the while the unfortunate person who had suffered the heart attack lay dying at the counter.

An incident of a rather different nature hit the horse racing world in 1987 when Lester Piggott, the most famous jockey of his era, appeared in court charged with tax evasion. The case, brought by HM Revenue and Customs, was rather aptly codenamed Centaur, of the half-man, half-horse beast of mythology.

In 1954 at just 18, Piggott had been the youngest jockey to win the Derby and went on to win the race nine times among 5,300 successes in over 30 countries.

His personal wealth was estimated to be in the region of £20million, and he was found guilty at Ipswich Crown Court of a tax fraud of over £3million in relation to undeclared earnings. In October 1987 he was sentenced to three years imprisonment. It was somewhat ironic that, before the court case, Piggott had reached an agreement with the HM Revenue and Customs for unpaid tax. Everyone was happy but then Piggott proceeded to write a cheque for the seven-figure sum on a bank account that had not previously been declared to the authorities – and they were not impressed. Using a cheque from the undisclosed bank account Piggott had stupidly signed his own confession of guilt.

*

The era should also be noted for the birth of a publication that would have a long-reaching impact. In April 1986 Sheikh Mohammed Bin Rashid Al Maktoum founded the *Racing Post* as a daily racing and sports betting paper to provide serious rivalry to *The Sporting Life*.

By the middle of the decade betting tax had reached 7.5%. In addition, the betting levy payment demanded by the horse racing authorities and supported by the government had reached such a level that betting shop operators were deducting 10% from winnings to pay these levies. Punters could choose whether or not to pay the 10% levy on their stakes when placing the bet. From a punter's point of view it was better to reduce the stake and pay the 10% tax rather than pay the tax on winnings.

For example, if a punter placed £100 on a horse whose odds were 2-1 he would receive £270 should the horse win (£100 @ 2-1 = £300 –

10% = £270). If, instead, the punter placed £90.90 and paid the £9.09 tax (10% of £90.90 = £9.09) he would receive £272.70, with no tax deductions for his £99.99 outlay.

In this example the difference may appear small, but it becomes more pronounced with higher stakes and greater odds. In the never-ending battle of punter versus bookmaker, the option for the punter of reducing the stake by 10%, but then paying the 10% tax levy with the bet, was a no-brainer. But few punters recognised, or took advantage of this edge, however slight.

A major effect of the high tax and horserace levy at this time was the increasing onset of illegal betting. It had long been known that bets were being taken by illegal bookmakers in pubs and clubs. There were various reasons for this: convenience for the punter in part, but the main driver was that the illegal bookmaker would not demand an additional payment of 10% of the stake with the bet, or make a 10% deduction from winnings. Not only was trade being lost by betting shop operators but the Chancellor of the Exchequer and horse racing were losing out.

Trade from high-rollers was also affected. With many high-turnover shops in my area I was constantly looking out for unprofitable trade and punters. Perhaps bizarrely, to a betting shop, an unprofitable punter could be losing money. On many occasions I would need to inform a shop manager, or tell the punter myself, often to his surprise, that his bets would no longer be taken.

A typical example would be a punter staking £50,000 during the previous three months and losing £3,000. Although the customer had lost £3,000 the bookmaker would need to pay over £4,000 in betting tax and horserace levy, thus ending up £1,000 down on the transactions. And this would be in addition to the effort and possible extra staff resource that would be needed to manage this part of the shop's business. Business from high-rollers needs careful managing and unfortunately this is often to the detriment of the regular profitable customers.

The decision to stop taking bets from a customer is never taken lightly. The bets would be examined and a judgement taken as to whether the selections were bad value each-way bets, where advantageous early prices were being obtained, bets on selections that were heavily tipped in the racing papers, or based on well informed inside information.

*

A distraction from the day-to-day problems came early in 1989 with a phone call that, with hindsight, served as an early warning of the road Mecca Bookmakers would soon travel. My area office was in City Road, directly opposite Companies House. The call was from Mecca's company secretary, asking me to complete a company search on the William Hill organisation, and to obtain the microfiche records of their business returns.

A request to obtain records from Companies House was not unusual, and it was often a precursor to Mecca making a bid for a company. Bob Green often said Mecca would one day either take over William Hill or William Hill would take over Mecca. It looked like that day was almost upon us.

*

Because the 1980s had brought live racing into betting shops and the horse race betting levy was still based on turnover, the amount raised had increased steadily and dramatically. By the end of decade the amount paid by betting shops to the levy was over £30million.

CHAPTER SEVEN

THE 1990S

Mecca/William Hill merger, Slow-count con,
Late-bet fraud, Civil-action injunctions, Hole-In-One gang,
Evening opening, National that never was, Derby changed to
Saturday, National Lottery 49s,Court case over £259,000
bet not paid, Grand National bomb scare, Football Stadium
lights, The *Racing Post* and the demise of *The Sporting Life*,
Wrong greyhound results published, Frankie Dettori's Seven
winners, Joe Coral, EPoS, Sunderland Eight,
Green Seal-IBAS-Tatts

By the end of 1989 Grand Metropolitan, which owned Mecca Bookmakers, had acquired the William Hill organisation. During that year, and leading up to the purchase, there were changes at Mecca including Grand Metropolitan placing their own people on the board. Anticipating a successful takeover, Grand Metropolitan wanted an influence on the newly merged company board

Following the merger of Mecca and William Hill the directors carried out an examination of cost-cutting synergies which was followed by a raft of redundancies – split equally between both companies.

The plan for the new company was to have a third of key jobs manned by Mecca staff, a third by William Hill staff and a third by personnel from outside the betting industry. Further, the cost-cutting exercise ensured there were far fewer staff than in the previous Mecca and Hills structures. The whole operational management structure for both companies was reorganised. I, and the other staff who had survived the cull, could describe the structure left in place in one word – chaos.

All the nationwide Mecca area offices, which carried out the administration, operational, security and fraud-detection functions were closed down, as was William Hill's central security department in Leeds. I was promoted from my area manager's role to regional security manager.

Over the following years this role expanded to include responsibility for over 700 betting shops, almost 50% of the company estate, together with a number of London-based departmental offices.

In the security department there were different responsibilities and procedures to learn, plus many more tasks to accomplish and fewer resources with which to accomplish them – a situation repeated through much of the newly formed company. Still, I always enjoyed a challenge!

*

Morale was poor. Bob Green and some of his fellow directors and senior executives left to seek new opportunities in America. Those staff that survived the cull were left wondering what sort of company they were now working for, having seen so many knowledgeable, hardworking and loyal colleagues made redundant. I remember the newly appointed chief executive of the time telling a gathering of staff that this was now a period of 'tough love'.

The low morale manifested itself in a high level of fraud. Imagine a shop manager and his staff seeing their experienced area manager made redundant only to be replaced by one who was contactable only by pager and freshly recruited from somewhere outside the industry, such as Woolworths. The management mantra that says you don't have to be able to drive a train to be chairman of Network Rail may be true, but this was too far. What was a shop manager to do when he had a bet query or a difficult situation to deal with?

Worse still, how could shop staff resist, for instance, the temptation to pay themselves out through a false lost ticket claim on a winning bet that had been gone unpaid in the shop for several weeks? Previously, knowing that the streetwise area manager would pick up on it would deter such a theft theft. Now it was open house.

The Mecca area offices, where shop staff could gain advice and information and where the security checking and auditing was carried out, were gone. It is little wonder that some shop staff, seeing their new, distant, inexperienced management, took advantage.

Bet stakes being under-rung intentionally, late bets processed where the winner was known, suspicious till cash discrepancies, faked robberies, banking not carried out followed by the shop manager disappearing and leaving no forwarding address, were just a few of the types of incident that the new regional security departments had to deal with and prevent. Though not new, the number of incidents reached new heights following the merger.

Every case of staff fraud was reported to police after an internal investigation carried out by myself and a security investigator. Some of my investigators were experienced senior betting shop operational staff and they brought a wealth of industry knowledge to the department. Others were retired Metropolitan police CID officers – in their early to mid 50s with a lot of working life left to give.

The ex-police officers taught us all about interview techniques. Body language, tell signs, psychology, statement taking, judges rules and, the role of the Crown Prosecution Service (CPS), evidence required to bring a successful prosecution and so on. Similarly these former police officers benefited from all of the experience that my experienced industry-savvy staff and I could provide.

Surprisingly, at this time the threat of being caught and subsequent prosecution did not seem to offer any deterrent. Or at least not to the majority of staff who were found out. Left with little actual or perceived supervision, a mixture of temptation, apathy, and an attitude of 'no one is bothered any more' seemed to kick in. This was in addition to those instances where desperation for money was the driver – remember that betting shops do not have as their stock sweets for the pick 'n' mix counter, but relatively large sums of ready cash.

I don't know whether it was the high incidence of fraud that my security department uncovered, or the sob stories that unfolded when the employee confessed, but certainly these times and my new expanded responsibilities took some getting used to. If a few of the many sob stories that I was told during the investigation reflected a semblance of truth, there are quite a number of people out there who live terribly sad lives.

After a while we in the security department became immune to the tales of woe that were thrown at us. But, thinking back, I don't know if becoming hard-hearted to a fellow human's plight is a good thing.

Ironically Christmas always brought a peak in staff fraud activity. Cashiers who were often single mothers, and who would want their child, or children, to have as good a Christmas as others, would succumb to temptation. Some managers, who would suffer from a moment of madness, would similarly fall to temptation to what they saw as apparently easy money to be had. Long-serving cashiers, who should have known better, often in collusion with smooth-talking gigolos (what a wonderful picture that term conjures up), were also prone to acting fraudulently. All who were caught were dismissed, referred to police, and their lives and reputations left in tatters, often for only relatively minimal sums.

It was at this time that I saw at close quarters the workings of the law-enforcement system in relation to betting shops. Liaison with police was vital in dealing with armed robberies, staff and customer fraud, but I was surprised at the high level of protection – all apparently in the interest of justice – afforded the defendant by law.

Rules of evidence, interview rules and human rights laws, together with the hassle that a witness has to endure should their evidence be required in court, all conspired (in my opinion) to work against justice being done. Even with weighty evidence but with the accused responding with 'no comment' and pleading not guilty, the CPS often decided it would not be in the public interest to have a trial because of the expense.

*

Defence lawyers were well paid from the public purse to put up a case and even when the accused was found guilty, or admitted guilt, the sentence meted out often seemed inadequate. Was this partly in the interests of cutting the expense of an increased prison population? I am sure that my colleagues in competing bookmaking firms felt the same. Lack of law enforcement often forced bookmakers to take civil action, with William Hill's head of security Dennis Burke leading the way.

The scourge of the slow-count was one problem the industry struggled with in the 1990s. The slow-count fraud is one where a betting slip is written out, normally for a greyhound race and, just before the off the slip is handed across the counter for the cashier to register through the till and microfilm camera.

Most betting shop counters would be thronged with customers trying to place bets in the last minute before a race is due to go off, as is the common culture among punters. In the rush to serve all customers on time, most staff prioritise taking and processing the bets offered, which involved registering the bets in the till and putting them through the security microfilm camera during the last-minute rush. Then, once the race had started, the cash would be taken from those who had placed bets but had yet to pay. Which is what the slow-count merchants sought to exploit.

The con was simple. Find a busy shop, write the bet, wait for the rush just before the start of the race, get the harried cashier to process the bet, then fumble around with the cash or go through the motion of counting the money out to oneself, or of checking the money. All this time the slow counter would be listening to, or watching, the race broadcast; if the greyhound written on the betting slip won, or looked likely to win, the stake would be quickly handed over.

The slow counter would know that the cashier would be thankful to receive the money in order for the till to be balanced. If the selection was losing, or looked like it would lose, the slow counter would leave the shop without paying for the bet, thus leaving the cashier with a discrepancy in the till.

With police unwilling to spend resources on taking action, Hills decided to concentrate the security department efforts on identifying the slow-count perpetrators and serving High Court injunctions against them.

It was a hard, time-consuming struggle to gather the evidence via statements and CCTV footage that would ensure a successful hearing in the High Court. It was also expensive.

Nevertheless, the security department was successful in having a High Court judge order that the identified slow-count gangs were kept out of William Hill shops. Failure to obey a High Court order would normally result in a prison sentence.

For Hills the problem of the slow-count con was solved and the grapevine told us other bookmakers were envious of what we had achieved, partly because they then experienced an increase in slow-count activity.

*

Even so, there was always the danger that other slow-count gangs would appear. Betting shop staff were constantly asked not to process the bet unless the stake was handed over. This mantra set the scene for another gang to cause havoc in the industry. At Hills we nicknamed them the 'Greek Team' as they were Mediterranean in appearance.

Their scam was to take advantage of the cashiers' fear that the money would not be given for a bet, and so they made a great play of handing over, in good time, the stake money. The well-mannered gang knew this would put the staff at ease, after which time they would use every ploy imaginable to delay handing the betting slip over and would only do so when the result of the race, usually a greyhound race, was known.

Another ploy was to put on the counter a bundle of betting slips, some of which would contain obscure events. To delay matters, prices would be requested for selections in these obscure events. During this process a betting slip containing the winning greyhound would surreptitiously be slipped in among the others still on the counter waiting to be processed.

Over time we discovered that the Greek Team were in fact Londoners from Stepney, Islington, Clapton and Stoke Newington. Again the police were unwilling to take action, so the William Hill security department took civil action and obtained a High Court injunction preventing them from entering one of our shops. As with the slow-counters, it was a long and expensive process but we got there in the end.

As described earlier, some punters use fraud and cheating to extract money unfairly while others use their shrewdness and knowledge to fight the fight with bookmakers. The 'Hole-In-One Gang' fell into this latter category. This pair from Essex had worked out – to the surprise of the uninitiated – that in 39 major golf tournaments there had been 30 holes-in-one.

Scoring a hole in one is the Holy Grail all golfers aspire to achieve, despite the custom that demands the player has to buy everyone in the clubhouse a drink. In the early 1990s many small betting shop owners had not realised that a professional player scoring a hole-in-one in a major tournament was not unusual. Perhaps blinded by the fact that although many shop owners and managers were golfers they had never scored one, they would offer what were in hindsight outrageously generous odds for this achievement.

They were not on their own in this foolishness. Back in the late 1970s, Ladbrokes, Hills and others were also unaware of how easy it was for professionals to achieve a hole-in-one at a tournament on a relatively easy course. On several occasions during this era, winning bets had been laid at odds from 10-1 to 40-1 when the true odds were more like evens.

But in the 1990s the Hole-In-One Gang from Essex were still getting odds of 100-1 or thereabouts for such a feat from some unenlightened betting shop operators who thought they had a pair of mugs on their hands. Little did the shop owners realise they were the mugs. Inevitably, when the bets won, some paid out and some refused and simply closed their businesses down instead.

The 1993 Grand National start fiasco.

Back in the world of horse racing there was an episode that affected every betting shop in Britain. On 3 April 1993, the fiasco labelled 'the Grand National that never was' took place.

The starter, Keith Brown, was officiating at his last Grand National and had difficulty in choosing the moment to start the race, so that the 39 horses were lined up and facing the right way. Trying to anticipate the off, a group of horses got too close to the starting tape and the starter, believing all was well, activated the handle that raised the tape.

Horses that were too close to the tape got caught up in it, beneath their heads and around their legs – part of it even got caught around the neck of jockey Richard Dunwoody. On one side of the course the tape lifted correctly and 30 of the horses raced off, while on the other side nine horses got caught up in the spoiled tape and did not start.

As the 30 horses galloped off, the starter waved his flag in an attempt to call them back. But his flag was unfurled so the recall man stationed further down the course was either unable to see, or did not react, to this recall signal.

Other attempts were made to stop the race, with officials frantically waving flags or simply waving. Although some of the jockeys who had raced off at the 'start' did pull up, others took little notice and raced on, stating afterwards that they believed the race was being stopped by protesters. Esha Ness, with a starting price of 50-1, crossed the finishing line first.

Coincidentally, John White, the jockey of Esha Ness, had John Buckingham, rider of Foinavon in 1967, as his valet that day. Once Esha Ness had gone past the finishing line Buckingham told White to get weighed in, just in case the race was declared valid, but chaos reigned.

There was talk of the nine who had not started taking part in a rerun race but after much debate the race that Esha Ness had won was declared a no race. The frustrated crowd booed officials and the starter in particular, who had to be escorted from the scene by police. What a shambles, witnessed by an estimated 300 million television viewers around the world. The 1993 Grand National was never run and the record books show it as a void race.

In betting shops there was much confusion. Settlers were waiting, seemingly forever, for an official announcement; punters who had backed Esha Ness demanded to be paid; others were demanding their money back on a void race. Meanwhile, other race results were coming in and other bets had to be dealt with. Eventually the announcement came through that the National would be declared void. Thus, one of the busiest days in the life of a betting shop became even busier when an estimated £75million wagered on the race had to be reprocessed and the stakes handed back.

Betting shops are forever evolving, but the announcement made two days earlier than the void Grand National, by Home Secretary Kenneth Clarke on 1 April 1993, was believed by some staff to be an April Fool's day joke. Following lobbying from the major bookmakers, Clarke announced that betting shops would be allowed to remain open in the evenings from April through to August.

Small independents were against the initiative as they feared there would be little trade to warrant the longer hours, and they worried about staffing the shops. Such organisations as the Greyhound Board of Great Britain had been against the change as they feared their business would suffer. Hats off yet again though, for the way that large betting shop organisations and trade association BOLA (now the ABB) were able to influence legislators.

The first evening horse meeting affected was at Taunton on 16 April. During the ensuing spring and summer there would be a further 133 evenings when betting shops could, and would, remain open.

August 1993 brought further deregulation for betting shops at the hands Michael Howard, then Home Secretary. Larger TV screens, adverts in shop windows and the availability of refreshments were some of the moves allowed.

This was followed by the announcement in May 1994 that, one year hence, betting shops would be allowed to open on certain Sundays. Over time, restrictions have been lifted and now betting shops can open throughout the year on Sundays and evenings.

As any in the betting shop industry who went through this change will confirm, the path to evening and Sunday opening was not an easy one. The vast majority of industry employees feared and initially resisted the changes. Not only staff in the shops but also staff in head office functions such as telephone betting, liability control, security and back office operations.

They worried about getting home following a late closing, and about their personal safety, on top of how to resolve child-care issues and disruption to family life.

Sunday opening brought additional worries, including from those with strong religious beliefs about working on the Sabbath. Most employers tried to address these concerns above and beyond the protection that employment law already gave. One such proviso of employment law was that no existing employee could be forced to work on a Sunday unless they had freely volunteered and had signed a contract to do so.

Although the majority of staff found the changes inconvenient or even unworkable, in truth many businesses such as pubs, cinemas, bingo halls and restaurants all employ staff to work unsocial hours. So one way or the other the betting industry was determined to meet the challenges and ensure that, where trade demanded, the shops would be staffed. The bottom line, unfortunately, was that if some staff left because of the changes then so be it. Many others would jump at the chance to fill the subsequent job vacancies.

It was always accepted that new and extra staff would need to be recruited and trained in order to deal with the additional trading hours. And gradually, existing staff started to volunteer to work the perceived unsocial hours, in order to earn extra salary. Nowadays many organisations use a four long days on, three days off rota and this system appears to suit most.

The ups and downs of the profitability of betting shops is a never-ending story. Thus the fillip that evening and Sunday opening gave to the industry was balanced by the introduction of the National Lottery in November 1994, which brought betting to a much wider audience as the public were allowed to buy lottery tickets. Lotteries were not new to the UK – the first such National Lottery was in 1569, but it ceased and was resurrected, on and off, between 1750 and 1826 when it again died out.

Camelot, the National Lottery organisers, promoted their game as one in which the public, from the age of 16, could donate via the purchase of a £1 ticket, to good causes. At the same time the ticket holder was buying into the opportunity of winning a prize that could be anything from £10 to millions of pounds.

It was interesting how the concept was marketed as a charitable and leisure pastime. The purchaser of a ticket was labelled as someone having a 'play', and the reward was winning a 'prize'. Any surplus money would go to 'good causes'.

The notion of 'play' and 'prize' had already been coined by the operators of Adult Gaming Centres (AGCs) but one could not criticise Camelot for using the same ploy. No matter how it is dressed up, the reality is that buying a National Lottery ticket is gambling.

The weekly draw, now called the Lotto, took place on a Saturday evening. There was no limit on how many tickets one could buy and over time instant-win scratch cards were also introduced. These are readily available in retail outlets, garages and supermarkets. There are also now midweek draws, and other 'games' with different win criteria for which further tickets can be purchased.

One wonders if the majority of people who buy these tickets do so with the priority, or even the thought, that they are giving to good causes. Or is it, just as in a betting shop, that they take part because they are buying into a dream, hoping that this maybe their lucky, life-changing day. 'It could be you,' says the catchy adverting slogan, rather than: 'Give to good causes'.

Betting shop owners soon noticed, following the introduction of the National Lottery, that their turnover and number of betting slips taken was dramatically decreasing. And why shouldn't they? The public's leisure pound, a discretionary spend, was now being attracted by an easily accessible, instant-win bet. One did not have to look for a fully licensed and regulated betting shop to place a bet. Anybody 16 years or over could just go to the local newsagent or petrol station and place a bet under the guise of the Lottery.

With a touch of irony, Licensed Betting Offices were not allowed to sell Lottery tickets. They were also not allowed to take bets on which numbers would be drawn and they are also out of bounds to anyone under the age of 18.

*

Trying to put one's point across to the government, in an attempt to change things, is not always the waste of time that some people perceive it to be. MPs do sometimes listen, and not just to hard lobbying. The year 1995 was a case in point. Betting shop staff were encouraged to write to their MPs pointing out the effect the Lottery and betting tax was having on trade and jobs in the industry.

It was at this time that I met former Prime Minister Edward Heath, who was my MP. Rather than write a letter I went to his surgery to make my case on behalf of William Hill. Despite being nearly 80 years old, he was very alert and aware of the issues I put to him, extremely approachable and very charming. I could not help but tell him the disappointment I felt when he lost the battle against the miners, in his 'who runs the country' election. As I left his surgery he said: 'we shall see what we can do', and followed this up with a letter confirming that he had sympathy with what I had said.

In that year's budget it was announced that betting tax would be reduced by 1% from 7.75% to 6.75%. Consequently deductions from returns were reduced from 10p to nine pence in the pound. Not a massive change but a move in the right direction, and I like to think my chat with a former Prime Minister helped.

And the main players in the betting industry decided to continue to fight back against the Lottery. They first tried to embarrass the government into letting them take bets on the Lottery and tried to show how illogical the policy was by taking bets on the Irish Lottery.

William Hill introduced the bet first on the Irish Lottery, called Lucky Choice. It offered the public better odds than they could achieve by buying a Lottery ticket. Although the government did not relent on its policy, Lucky Choice was nevertheless a real money-spinner for the shops.

Another major change in 1995 was the organisers of the Derby made a radical change and switched the race from a Wednesday to a Saturday – despite much public angst.

The Derby had been run on Epsom Downs since 1780 when the Earl of Derby and Sir Charles Bunbury had flipped a coin to decide what it should be called. If the coin had landed heads the race would have been called the Bunbury. Instead the coin landed as tails and the Earl of Derby won the privilege of naming the race, which Bunbury's horse, Diomed, won.

The running of the Derby on the first Wednesday in June had become as much a British tradition as roast beef on a Sunday, fish and chips on a Friday and pancakes on Shrove Tuesday. The Derby used to stop the nation; Parliament rose and factories, pubs, clubs and offices took coach and open-topped bus parties on to Epsom Downs. Others would gather around radios or televisions and those workers who had not taken the day off to go to the race, crammed into betting shops to hear the outcome. It was a national institution.

Derby day in my years as an area manager in the City of London was a great day. Some shop managers would organise a running buffet lunch for their staff who were unable to move from the tills. All day, before the race, the cashiers would be frantically taking bets and helping those ever-present once-a-year punters. After the race, the cashiers would then be busy serving those who were fortunate enough to have picked the winner or one of the placed horses. In thanks for all of their hard work I would organise a disco with food, drinks and free raffle in the evening at a local pub for the area's shop staff.

But in 1995 the race had a new sponsor in Vodafone. And in an effort to attract the attention of a worldwide audience who were at their leisure on Saturday, the race was switched.

The move has not proved unanimously popular and the race now gets lost among all the sporting events that take place over the first weekend in June. That 1995 Saturday running of the Derby was won by Lammtarra in a then record time of 2mins 32.31secs. Maybe the air has more oxygen in it on a Saturday.

Returning to the National Lottery, in 1996 the multiple betting shop owners saw that, as with the Irish Lottery, the returns to the public, at around 45%, were poor compared with betting with a bookmaker – where the return to punters is around 80%. The remaining 55% of turnover from the National Lottery was either kept as profit for the organisers and retailers, given as a tax to the government, given to the body responsible for distributing to good causes, or put aside for periodic 'super draws'. The thought was that the bookmaking industry could offer the public a similar betting opportunity but offer better odds.

Thus, in 1996, the not-for-profit company 49s Ltd was formed

Lammtarra and Frankie Dettori.

and the 49s bet was born, offering punters the opportunity to bet on balls drawn from a drum, just as with the National Lottery. The title 49s came from the number of balls from which the winning numbers were drawn. Draw machines and balls identical to the ones used by the National Lottery were purchased and installed in a TV studio at SIS headquarters in London. New betting shop signage was installed with the emphasis on highlighting the difference in odds in comparison with the National Lottery. Draws on the 49s game were daily and it was an instant hit with the public.

The initiative was so popular that Camelot took the betting industry to court in an attempt to ban it. But the court took the view that 49s was not a lottery but a fixed-odds bet and therefore quite legal for betting shops to take. A resounding victory then, with Camelot ordered to pay the betting industry's court costs.

Not only was the equilibrium between betting and the lottery restored, but trade in general increased, along with the number of women using betting shops. It seemed the National Lottery had sanitised betting, made it more acceptable and introduced a new audience to having a flutter.

The episode also reminded the industry that one should always try to turn a negative situation into a positive one – a good maxim for business or personal life.

*

Another initiative sparked by the National Lottery was that William Hill arranged a contract to sell lottery tickets from kiosks installed in shopping centres, under the name Norwich Enterprises. Although business was brisk, the commission paid for selling the tickets was barely enough to cover the cost of rent and staff. William Hill hoped to sell advertising space on the kiosks to make the venture worthwhile but it was soon decided the kiosks were not a long-term prospect and they were sold off.

As I have said before, life is full of ups and downs, and the betting industry will always remember Saturday 28 September 1996 as one of those 'down' days. I was putting the final touches to the 21st birthday party preparations 0f my son Jon-Paul when my office called to ask whether I had heard that Frankie Dettori had gone through the card at Ascot that day, riding all seven winners. I hadn't, because I had been busy with no time for TV that day.

Sir Gordon Richards had ridden six out of six winners at Chepstow in 1933, but no jockey had notched up seven out of seven, a terrific achievement on such a high-quality Ascot card.

Although Dettori was a popular jockey no one realised just how popular he was with the betting public until the telephones in the betting shops started to ring after his first two winners that day. The trebles, accumulators, yankees and other multiple bets, all with Dettori's mounts as the selections, were now well and truly running and these betting slips were being put to the top of the settlers' piles in shops across Britain.

Still, even after two winners no one could visualise what was to

Frankie Dettori wins on Fujiyama Crest, the seventh win of his 'magnificent seven' at Ascot.

happen that afternoon. Dettori's first ride, Wall Street, had come in at 2-1, Diffident then obliged at 12-1 and Mark Of Esteem was the next success at 100-30. Decorated Hero followed at 7-1 and already the payout total had reached many millions of pounds and there were still three races to go. Fatefully, winning at 7-4, followed next, then Lochangel at 5-4 and finally, with the BBC's Grandstand programme halting its broadcasts from other events, all media attention switched to Ascot's seventh and final race.

Fujiyama Crest had been given little chance by the racing correspondents in the morning papers and before the on-course bookmakers opened their betting he was quoted at 12-1. Thanks to the mountain of money that was running on to him in accumulators, the price of Fujiyama Crest was slashed when betting at the course opened and he was sent off at 2-1.

The first six winners had already produced accumulative odds of over 8,365-1 and the betting shop representatives tried desperately to get money back to the course to be placed on Fujiyama Crest in an effort to tighten his odds as much as possible.

*

Some on-course bookmakers considered that this true 12-1 chance still had the same likelihood of winning as he had at the start of the day, and concluded that the romantic tale of a young, charismatic Italian riding all seven winners at such a high-class meeting as this Ascot card surely would not, could not, happen.

Some on-course bookmakers were therefore prepared to lay Fujiyama Crest and take on the off-course bookmakers. To attract as much money as possible they would not go shorter than 2-1 and some, who saw this as a golden opportunity to make a killing, offered 3-1 and even 4-1, and for large sums.

The bookmaker Gary Wiltshire was one who considered that even with Dettori on board Fujiyama Crest would still run only as fast as a true 12-1 chance should. How wrong he proved to be and what fortunes he and others lost that day. Wiltshire lost £500,000 to Coral alone and over £1million in total. Like most who try to make a living in this strange game he took it on the chin, raised the cash, paid up and continues to be a force to be reckoned with and a welcome character in the racecourse betting ring.

Dettori was responsible for a seven-horse accumulator that paid £25,095 to a £1 stake at starting prices. This figure increased dramatically if the morning prices offered in betting shops had been taken. Unfortunately for those shops, many punters did take the early prices. As an example, if just the one early price of 12-1 had been taken on Fujiyama Crest in the £1 seven-horse accumulator the punter would have received £108,751 for his £1 instead of £25,095.

So the hordes of punters who follow the top jockeys, usually considered to be mugs by the bookmakers, had their day of glory. Dettori's Magnificent Seven is estimated to have cost the industry in excess of £30million.

The senior management team at William Hill were called to an emergency meeting to discuss how to ensure winning bets would be paid with the minimum of fuss. Banking arrangements for shop managers to obtain cash had to be organised, normal security procedures regarding bets with substantial winnings had to be rethought, and other contingencies considered.

There was an air of gloom in anticipation of a large chunk of company profits being wiped out overnight and with it any bonus that might have been paid to us that year. Nevertheless, and because no one else seemed about to say it, I said loud and clear that: 'In the main, the cash will come back to us across the counter and it is vital that the shop managers pay up with a smile'.

It was something I had picked up from Connor's many years previously. My old guv'nor, Con, always said when having to pay out on a large winning bet: 'Pay up with a smile and give the impression there's lots more cash where that came from. Don't let them see you're hurting. They'll come back for more and we'll get it back in the end.'

It was the case that William Hill, indeed the industry, would be judged by how efficiently the winning bets were paid on the Monday morning when doors opened for business. We were aware the media were looking for betting shops to slip up and were ready for any eventuality. There were no dramas and every punter got his winnings in cash or by cheque without having to wait ... and life went on.

So on the day when the Samuels clan was due to celebrate my son's 21st birthday I was at the meeting at William Hill headquarters that lasted for most of the day. I had to leave my wife, daughter and son to look after our guests at home. I knew everything was in safe hands, with Robert my son-in-law coming up trumps by stepping in to oversee the bar, and I did manage to get back in time to enjoy some of the party. For more than one reason, and with some sarcasm, I say: 'Thanks a lot Frankie'.

Dettori later bought Fujiyama Crest, retired him as a gesture of thanks and kept him as the family pet. I wonder what some bookmakers would have done if they had got their hands on him instead?

For some organisations, Dettori's success had long-term repercussions and it was rumoured that the sale of Coral to Ladbrokes 14 months later was because parent company Bass did not want to experience another trading day like it.

Coral Eurobet, as it is now known, was founded by Joseph Kagarlitsky

A Coral shop in the 1960s. You can just read the notice inside the window: 'Never a quarrel, bet with Coral'. Note the flyblown door curtain and the only recognition of the need for fresh air, an extractor fan stuck on the glass window above the door. Note also that this is a Turf and Football Accountant.

in 1926. He was born in Warsaw on 11 December 1904 and changed his name to Coral when he set up in business. Joe Coral had financial interests in speedway tracks and operated as an on-course bookmaker at greyhound courses. He cut his bookmaking teeth taking bets in snooker clubs in the 1920s, and in his later years he could still be seen playing snooker in the Victoria Club. He applied for British citizenship in 1952 and, after some consideration, including the concern that he had not divulged 39 previous driving offences on his application form, it was granted. One Home Office official commented: "For a bookmaker from Stoke Newington he's not a bad sort of fellow." Joe died in 1996, the same year as Dettori's great success.

Coral's early trading motto was: 'Never a quarrel, bet with Coral'. This motto may have been relevant in the days when the on-course bookmakers operated on the basis of 'my word is my bond' and most betting disputes were relatively straightforward. This, however, was not the case as betting shops began to expand the markets on which they bet and more complicated issues came to the fore. The motto was dropped soon after the opening of betting shops, which may be just as well given the tale now to be told.

Mentioned earlier, microfilm cameras are perhaps the most vital part of a betting shop's security. Operators rely on what is recorded in their cameras and, though it often goes unnoticed, this reliance is enshrined in betting shop operating rules.

In September 1996 a betting shop customer discovered, not for the first time, that the bet is not what is shown on the betting slip receipt nor what the punter has in his hand, but rather that which has been recorded on the betting shop security microfilm camera.

A £50 correct-score football accumulator was placed in a Coral shop in Cardiff. The odds on the four-team correct-score bet produced a potential return of over £259,000. But there was no record of the bet on the shop microfilm so, after an enquiry, the bookmaker refused to pay out.

Although rare, it was not unprecedented that a bet could not be verified on a bookmaker's security system. Two reasons for this are that a mistake has been made and the employee has unintentionally failed to put the bet through the system or that the employee has deliberately not put the bet through and the winning selections have been written on the bet after the result is known.

The dispute caused quite a stir and was publicised by many newspapers. The customer took to demonstrating his anger at events nationwide. In turn Coral announced concern at the bona fides of the bet.

The customer took the case as far as he could in law, requesting that the matter be dealt with by way of the Arbitration Act 1979. This provided a process whose findings are enforceable in law, but his request was refused by the judge who heard the initial demand, and again by another judge when the customer appealed.

At the time the transaction was made such bets were not recognised as contracts in law, under the Gaming Act 1845. Therefore the dispute could not be heard in a civil court, neither could it be dealt with under the provisions of the Arbitration Act. The customer eventually had no choice but to give up on his claim.

Back to horse racing and the Grand National of 1997 was yet another that made front-page headlines, but for the wrong reasons. Two coded bomb warnings were received, reportedly from the IRA, which the police took seriously enough to have the meeting abandoned and the course at Aintree evacuated of all 60,000 spectators, horses, jockeys and officials. The race was run on the following Monday with free admission for all and was won by the 14-1 chance Lord Gyllene. So more hard work for betting shop staff, although the repercussions were not as severe as for the 1993 National.

Security was becoming more and more of an issue in the 1990s, not just for racecourses and businesses in general but, for many reasons, in betting shops. So security initiatives and innovations were researched, improved and then installed across the industry although even now, in some districts, when one walks into a betting shop it feels like going back to the 1960s.

The security changes were driven by the realisation that robbers saw betting shops as soft targets and were ignoring banks and building societies, which had installed effective crime-prevention measures.

Meanwhile marketing men were convincing betting industry directors that their shops could be made more welcoming, and trade would be increased, by removing the counter security screens. The phenomenon known as steaming soon manifested itself. Mainly in London, teenage gangs were jumping over betting shop counters, threatening staff with knives and stealing whatever cash they could.

*

Eventually, the industry listened to its security departments and counter screens were re-installed. Even so, armed robberies were still prevalent. Strangely, some parts of the UK were unaffected by armed robberies and steaming, while in others, mainly inner-cities, they were becoming an everyday fact of life.

Time-lock safes which opened only at predetermined times where installed to help deter robbers. If managed properly the safes would ensure a minimal amount of cash was available.

Overt and covert CCTV cameras linked to recording systems were installed. Some allowed the scene to be monitored from a central station. Pictures of the perpetrators could be sent immediately over a secure internet to laptops installed in patrolling police cars – an initiative led by Ladbrokes security, headed by Dave Georgeson and colleagues Peter Brewin and Neil Harris.

At William Hill I helped instigate and deliver a training programme called Counter Plan that empowered staff to deal effectively and appropriately with incidents. It was the brainchild of the crime-prevention unit of the Metropolitan Police Flying Squad, and rolled out across William Hill's entire UK estate, resulting in great success in the war against robbers.

Silent and audible alarms were installed, that allowed staff to call police at the touch of a button. Electronic locks were fitted to entrance doors, allowing controlled entry to, and exit from, the shop.

The main trade association of the industry, the ABB, introduced an initiative to allow members to put up a reward of up to £10,000 for anyone who gave information that assisted police in a prosecution. Many tens of thousands of pounds have been paid from this fund and many offenders have found themselves behind bars as a result.

Risk assessments were carried out to help identify security weak spots and, depending on circumstances and local environment, relevant changes were made. These included the fitting of wide-angle mirrors to cover blind spots, personal attack alarms, counter-to-ceiling glass security screens, smart water, mobile guards, cash collections by security guards, restricted opening and closing times and other initiatives on which it would not be prudent to elaborate here.

Every day was different but exciting and challenging. Just one of many incidents that comes to mind was a burglary at the Ascot branch. I overheard the telephone report come through from the manager to my security department and thought 'just another burglary, wonder how much damage was caused to the shop'. More often than not a burglar would cause damage in getting into the shop and then possibly vent his anger on the equipment inside once he realised there was no easy money to be had since it was all locked away in a secure safe.

But this burglary was different. The manager reported that the shop had been broken into, the burglar alarm had been totally disarmed, the alarm link to the police monitoring company had been circumvented, the CCTV had been trashed and there was a large hole where the safe should be.

The safes that are installed in most shops are fireproof and bombproof. Their bottoms are fitted with metal girders and then the safe is deep buried into the floor with cement and concrete, and fitted with one or two other surprises.

Despite these measures the safe containing an unusually large sum of cash, just over £40,000, had been taken. The previous day, the William Hill betting unit in the (old) grandstand at Ascot had enjoyed an unusually profitable day, but normal banking procedures could not be carried out as the staff had mislaid the unit's night safe wallets. As a result, the unit was 'stuck' with a much larger sum of cash than normal and it had been transferred to the safe of the nearby betting shop. Subsequently, overnight, you can guess the rest. The police investigation and our own internal investigation had many twists and turns. Many theories were put forward as to why, on this night of all nights, this shop suffered such a professional and well-planned attack.

Nearly every burglary we suffered was committed by juveniles who thought there may be a few notes left in the tills. Often the alarm ringing was enough to frighten them off.

My own theory, and one that was shared by police, was that a local professional villain or gang had lost most of what the betting unit had won, and were determined to get their cash back. The gang probably followed the money at the end of the meeting, planning to attack the staff at the night safe vault, but changed the plan to carry out the burglary when it was taken to a nearby shop.

Police did obtain some good CCTV images of vehicles using the road immediately outside the shop and no doubt had their own theories as to who the culprits were.

The reason why I mention this incident, apart from the uniqueness, is that some 30 years earlier, while working for City Tote, I had managed this branch and the visit to the shop to investigate the burglary brought back vivid memories of those times.

The shop layout was exactly as I had remembered it. Thirty years earlier, on a Boxing Day morning with the snow falling fast and seemingly the rest of the world still asleep and getting over their Christmas celebration, I had received a call from head office asking if I would go to Ascot to open and manage the branch as the manager had reported sick.

From East London where I lived at the time, to Finsbury Park to collect the spare shop keys, then on to Waterloo to catch whatever train might be running to Ascot. It turned into a three-hour trip to get to the shop and I only saw maybe four or five punters all day long as racing had been cancelled due to the weather.

But the show must go on was the motto and I enjoyed the train ride through the Surrey countryside, which looked particularly spectacular with the snow falling on the grass and trees. The journey did open up a new world to me and it was on that train that I promised myself that my wife and I would move to this part of the country and bring our family up in these leafy suburbs. Not necessarily Virginia Water but somewhere not too dissimilar. Only a few years later we bought a house in the lovely area of Farnborough, Hampshire.

Ascot was our local racecourse and we spent many a happy day there, enjoying the late Autumn meetings best. There would be coal-fired braziers scattered around the course warming any spectators who felt the need. My baby son would be cosily tucked up in his pram, with a hot water bottle on one side of him and wrapped up hot sausage sandwiches on the other side. My young daughter liked looking at the horses and we all enjoyed listening to the Army band that often played.

*

As well as security, we had other, bizarre problems while trying to raise service levels in betting shops. For instance, public toilets are now commonly found in betting shops, but how does one deal with the suspicion of drug abuse activity in the facilities? We installed specialist neon light fittings that made it difficult for veins to be found and needles to be used.

After fitting comfortable seating there would be a suspicion of drug dealing in the shop. To deal with this we often removed all of the posters in the window so that passers-by could see in, overt CCTV cameras were fitted, extra lighting was installed and any blind spots were removed. Also the local police and/or community support officers, as part of their beat patrol, were asked and encouraged to visit the shop.

*

During the late 1990s many betting shops went through massive changes of ownership. George Walker's company Brent Walker, the new owners of the William Hill organisation, had gone under due to a mountain of debt. The debt was mainly due to Walker paying a huge price to Grand Metropolitan to obtain William Hill.

Following the completion of the deal, when the price Walker had paid was disclosed one financial expert commented: 'Someone has done a great deal here but I cannot work out yet who it is, time will tell'. Bob Green, who had gone to America by this time, was known to have put bids in for the William Hill/Mecca Bookmakers group, the empire that he had developed. However once the price required became, in Green's opinion, unviable, he dropped out of the bidding. Not surprisingly, within a short period of time, his judgement proved right once again. Many financial pundits, at the time of Brent Walker's collapse, believed the purchase of William Hill to be a deal too far.

Following the demise of Brent Walker there were many suitors for William Hill, which was eventually sold to Nomura, who in turn formed The Grand Bookmaking Company.

As mentioned earlier, Ladbrokes had bought Coral in December 1997, giving the new conglomerate a combined total of over 2,700 shops. With William Hill at 'only' just over 1,500 shops, Ladbrokes had put themselves in an unassailable position of being the biggest betting shop operator. Within a short while however the (then) Monopolies and Mergers Commission became interested in the Ladbrokes-Coral deal, and eventually declared the deal could not go ahead so the companies remained under separate ownership.

The Coral group was sold off to a management buyout backed by Morgan Grenfell Private Equity. Soon after the Coral group bought the internet business Eurobet and the firm has since traded under the name Coral Eurobet. A further management buyout was arranged in September 2002 with the backing of Charterhouse Development Capital

*

On 12 May 1998 *The Sporting Life*, the newspaper which had been displayed on the walls of betting shops since they had been legalised in 1961 and which enjoyed huge credibility with the betting and racing public, published for the final time.

Since its birth in April 1986 the *Racing Post* had been gaining ground on the *Life* and, crucially, had been listening to what the owners of betting shops wanted. When considering that the UK's 10,000 betting shops took at least three copies of *The Sporting Life* per day for customer and staff use, this was an important market.

The betting industry wanted a paper they could easily display on the walls of their shops. It had to have the form laid out in a way that would make it user-friendly, so that the form for a meeting shown on one page did not continue on to the back of the same page. It also wanted an improved marker sheet for their betting shop settlers.

The Racing Post listened, took action and gave betting shop owners what they wanted. *The Sporting Life* did little to respond and over time increasing numbers of shops took the *Racing Post* instead. Sales of *The Sporting Life* dwindled and in 1998 the paper's owner, the Trinity Mirror Group, made a deal with Sheikh Mohammed who had funded the *Racing Post*. The two papers merged under the title of the *Racing Post* and the *Life* ceased publication as a newspaper, but continued a presence online.

With the *Racing Post* therefore the prime source of sports and racing results for the betting industry, an unfortunate episode occurred on Monday 24 August 1998 when four incorrect greyhound results were reported for the Saturday evening meetings at Reading and Yarmouth.

Bets had been placed in shops throughout East London, Essex and Humberside on the four greyhounds from the evening meetings of 22 August. The results published in the *Racing Post* showed as winners three of the greyhounds that had not won. The fourth, which had won, was shown with a much-inflated starting price.

Although a few of the bets were paid early on the Monday morning, many shop managers where the bets had been taken became suspicious of the unusual winning bets involving these two small provincial greyhound stadiums. Checks were made and it was discovered that the four results were incorrect.

It was obvious that this was intentional fraud rather than a simple error, and the *Racing Post* hierarchy reported the matter to police who concentrated their efforts on finding the culprit at the newspaper's offices. But police soon discovered that the Post was not the only newspaper using the integrated computer system installed on several floors of Trinity Mirror's Canary Wharf office.

The unsuccessful scam could have netted in excess of £50,000 and data published in the *Racing Post* has since been made much more secure. The culprits were never brought to justice.

During the early 1990s betting tax had increased to 8% on stakes – the highest it had ever reached. There was also the mandatory contribution to the Horserace Betting Levy Board, which was at a cripplingly high level, resulting in deductions of 10% being made from punters' returns or stakes to compensate.

Not surprisingly trade in the shops was diminishing, and it was not going to bookmakers at the racecourse. The National Lottery wasn't the only thing to affect the betting shop industry – illegal betting in pubs, clubs, by telephone and even in betting shop-style premises was rife. The industry was trying to convince the government that the level of tax and levies was driving betting underground, to the detriment of all but those who run such unregulated set-ups.

The warning sirens about illegal gambling were falling on deaf government ears. Again the William Hill organisation, under the initiative of managing director John Brown, decided to take action. Brown considered that betting shops had no right to install spirit optics or beer pumps on its shop counters, so why, he mused, should pubs be allowed to give their customers the option of placing a bet while drinking.

It was known that approaches to the police or customs officials would be met with little action, so Brown tasked his head of security, Chris Bird, to take such action as was necessary to stop the illegal practice of bets being taken in pubs. Bird and Brown came up with a plan to gather evidence and then apply to licensing magistrates to have the licence of the relevant pub landlord revoked.

Security and operational staff were asked to look out for illegal betting activity in pubs in their vicinity. We did not have to wait long before reports started to pour in to the William Hill regional security departments. The first task was to prioritise them, to compare how much trade had decreased in nearby betting shops over the previous year or six months; then to pay a visit to the pub to gauge the level of illegal betting activity. My fellow investigators and I spent many a Saturday afternoon, over a pint or two, monitoring, or trying to identify, betting activity in pubs. A dirty job but somebody had to do it.

We were often shocked at the level of betting activity in pubs. Often it would be a case of the illegal bookmaker sitting in a corner, with the nearby television broadcasting the major horse race meeting of the day. On a table in front of him, the illegal bookmaker would have the racing papers of the day spread out, together with betting slips and maybe a numbering machine – a small cottage industry inside the pub and a microcosm of a legal betting shop. All that was missing was the constraints of legislation and regulation and, importantly, the need to pay taxes or levies.

If the level of betting activity was low, we would often simply remind the landlord of the licensing law and report the matter to the local licensing officer. But other, more serious, cases were dealt with by sending in a team with covert recording equipment. Some of the images obtained from these visits were astounding: betting on a large scale, under-age drinking and youngsters aged no more than ten playing at pool tables.

These cases were taken to court and the landlords lost their licences. As with the slow-count teams it was a long, hard slog and an expensive exercise. News soon spread of William Hill's success – and our action proved invaluable in early 2001 when the betting industry was trying to convince the government it should change the whole betting tax regime.

*

The IT revolution of the late 1990s brought another major change to the industry. For the previous 30 years betting shops had used tills, microfilm cameras and settlers with a quick mathematical brain to process bets. There had been some progress in the process of calculating winning bets with the introduction of desktop settlement machines. But these machines needed the operator to have a good working knowledge of how the bet was constructed or required the operator to undergo a comprehensive training programme. And none of these glorified calculators took into account bookmakers' rules, off-times or the accuracy of odds given.

The onset of reliable image-scanning equipment and software that could be programmed to understand betting terminology was the catalyst for change. In addition, computers that could carry out complicated calculations in a second were now cheaply available and telecom modems could transmit data immediately. All of this encouraged Electronic Point of Sale (EPoS) manufacturers to try to supply their wares to betting shops.

Ladbrokes were first out of the traps when they installed their bespoke EPoS system, labelling it their Shop 2000 initiative. Others followed, usually employing a system designed and provided by the IT company Alphameric. The system is sometimes referred to as a bet-capture system.

In the process the customer still writes out the bet but just a single copy of the slip is handed to the cashier. That slip is pre-printed with a barcode that the cashier puts through a scanner, while simultaneously registering the stake given on the till.

The EPoS system then automatically produces a scanned copy of the slip which contains printed details produced by the till terminal, such as the slip number, date, time, till terminal identification number and the amount of stake recorded by the cashier. This scanned copy is given to the customer as a receipt. It also serves as a record for the customer of what was written on the slip.

As with the old till and microfilm camera system, the customer is quickly served but then the work starts for the employee. All the bet details on the slip have to be recorded into the branch bet-capture computer. This part of the process is called translating the bet. The selection, the type of bet and the stake all have to be input.

The results will be sent by head office to the branch computer. If the bet has money to be paid on it the branch computer will recognise this and calculate the amount. The customer can produce his receipt, it will be put into the EPoS terminal – this part of the process is called 'dipping the slip' – and the terminal will recognise the barcode and display how much is to be paid to the customer.

At close of business the terminal will automatically calculate how much it has taken, how much it has authorised to pay, and what cash there should therefore be in the till. Overnight all the bet details taken during the day and the scanned images will be relayed to head office. The security department will view the images of any bets still to be paid and compare this to the details that have been input by the staff.

Security will be looking for input translations that differ from what is on the image of the bet and that which has been translated. If there are discrepancies they will be corrected, with the consequence that wrong payments can be stopped before the shop reopens. These translation errors are often found for large and small amounts, and are a major benefit of having an EPoS system.

Bearing in mind that EPoS is blind and relies on the information input by staff, many organisations get their security departments to trawl through the bets that have been paid to see if they have been translated, input and paid correctly in relation to the scanned image which the head office will be able to view. When errors are found a decision will be made as to whether they are genuine mistakes or deliberate fraud.

For instance, there might be a bet on a greyhound race where the scanned image shows it to be a forecast on trap numbers three and five. But when the translation is seen it shows that traps three and six were input as the forecast bet, and indeed traps three and six was the result. The EPoS system might then reveal that the translation of traps three and six was made after the race was run and the bet was paid as a winner on traps three and six.

Bets translated into the EPoS system after the selections have run is not an unusual occurrence as the priority for shop staff is to serve customers who are waiting at the counter. Once the rush is over the translations begin. So it is inevitable that some bets are translated into the system after the selections on the bet have run.

The security departments of the betting industry were often told by directors and senior operational staff that the onset of the EPoS system would be the death knell of our departments. They believed the introduction of EPoS would cure all ills. Having seen EPoS showcased at betting shop exhibitions we knew otherwise and laughed at their naivety – and could foresee the loopholes others couldn't.

One downside of the introduction of the EPoS system is that it has tended to dumb down the skills of betting shop staff. At one time every manager would know how to manually settle a bet and could explain to a customer how a dead-heat or a rule 4 deduction worked, and how a winning bet had been calculated. Such skills are now a rarity and just as the character in the TV comedy Little Britain would tell the customer 'computer says no' in the betting shop it is 'screen says £9.74', with the cashier having no idea how that sum has been reached.

Undoubtedly, though, there are benefits. Punters can be assured their bet has been settled correctly. For the company, some early warning of liabilities can be established, accurate data on types of bets taken can be gathered, a great benefit when it is remembered that levy is payable only on horse racing.

*

The golden future however lies in another type of EPoS process called marksense or quickslip, similar to that used by the National Lottery. In essence, the EPoS terminal can identify and automatically translate the instructions on the marksense betting slip. For now the slip is used only for football bets and single bets on popular events such as the Grand National and Derby.

The marksense slip typically has columns of blank squares. All the customer has to do is to mark, by way of a small line, the appropriate column, and stake box that corresponds to the bet he wants to place. So, for a bet on the Grand National, the slip would already be printed with the race name. There would be numbers running down the slip, top to bottom one to 40, which would represent the horse numbers. Simply by putting a line in the box that represents the horse number to be backed, a line in the appropriate stake box, then a line in the win or each-way box, the slip would be completed.

Once the slip is handed to the cashier the EPoS system would recognise the marks on the slip, translate it into the bet acceptance system and the customer would receive a printed version of the translation. Betting shop operators and staff love these slips as they do not need to be manually translated. Soon, the old method of punters writing out their slips will be a distant memory.

For now, though, let's stay with the past and an old-fashioned puzzle. Just before the millennium, on Tuesday 16 November 1999, there was a rarity that rivalled Dettori's Magnificent Seven – I suppose one could call it the Sunderland Eight. Tucked away in the northeast of England, and soon to be bought by the William Hill organisation, Sunderland greyhound stadium was the scene of a highly unusual event. Greyhounds running from trap six won the first eight races of the 12-race afternoon card. Bookmakers and the betting public were amazed as race after race the number six dog romped home.

Something was obviously amiss with the racing surface but the track authorities seemed slow to put whatever it was right. The on-course bookmakers were the first to react when, after the first three races, they made the opening price of trap six in the fourth race 3-1 rather than the expected 7-1. Trap six duly won the fourth race by nearly three lengths at a starting price of 5-2.

A similar scenario occurred in the next four races, with on-course bookmakers ignoring the tissue odds (devised by a form expert and used by bookmakers for their opening show) and instead offered odds of evens or thereabouts for trap six.

They were wise to do so as the next four races all went to the outside trap and on-course betting then collapsed into farce when, in the ninth race, the bookmakers offered trap six at 1-2, with all the other five greyhounds on offer at 10-1. But this time, action was taken before the start of the race. A tractor was brought on to the track and the whole running surface was raked and smoothed. Trap four won the ninth race, with trap six finishing second from last. Trap six did not win again in the last three races.

What had happened? The theory was that the ground on the inside and middle of the track had not been maintained and prepared for racing properly, with the consequence that it was cut up and rough. Some thought that part of the track had been over watered to make it muddy, while the outside of the track was a smooth, fast surface.

Punters and bookmakers at the track did not have to wait long to find out what was going on. It was soon learnt that a bet of four x £50 trebles and a £50 accumulator, tax paid, had been placed in a nearby betting shop on trap six winning the first four races. With the first four winners starting at 4-1, 9-2, 4-1 and 5-2 the bet produced a potential payout of £44,937.

There was an internal enquiry at the stadium closely followed by enquiries from the Bookmakers Afternoon Greyhound Service (BAGS), National Greyhound Racing Club (NGRC) and an investigation by the police. With a bet that stood to win almost £45,000 brought into the equation, it was obvious to expect skulduggery. But none of the investigations uncovered sufficient evidence to prove what had happened to the track was by design and not just happenstance.

Despite circumstantial evidence that there may have been malpractice, the NGRC declined to declare the meeting void and allowed the results to stand. Consequently, the record books show that trap six had indeed won all of the first eight races. Bets that had been won and lost at the course on the day stood, as did those placed off-course.

The shop that had taken the bet on trap six winning the first four races initially refused to pay the £45,000 winnings, so the customer took the dispute to the Independent Betting Arbitration (now Ajudication) Service (IBAS). After looking into the matter and noting that no action was taken by the police and NGRC, the IBAS ruled the winnings must be paid. A bitter pill to swallow for the betting shop, which paid the customer £45,000.

It was another incident that showed the potential vulnerability of betting shops. If there was malpractice it had not been orchestrated by bookmakers, but severely disadvantaged those punters who were not in on the information of what had happened to the track. They were instead relying on form to place bets, with the consequence that they lost their money.

IBAS is the organisation that bookmakers and their customers can use to adjudicate in a betting dispute. Its predecessor was the Green Seal service provided by *The Sporting Life*, which gave opinions on how a bet should be settled. It got its title because anyone wishing to use the service had to enclose the small green stamp that appeared on the top of the newspaper's front page. Although one never saw the details of the actual dispute, Sporting Life published the response from the Green Seal team, that would read as follows:

JS (Hartlepool). Your bet of three doubles and a treble has been settled correctly by the bookmaker. The total stake should have been £4 and not the 40p you wrote in the total stake box, paid and received a receipt for. Plus, your first two selections had already run and had won by the time you placed the bet.

One can probably guess the gist of the claim from JS of Hartlepool.

Once *The Sporting Life* ceased publication in May 1998 the betting industry was left with a void in the area of dispute resolution. Tattersalls Committee had long existed as a body to which disgruntled punters could take their case but it dealt only with horse racing disputes involving on-course bookmakers.

Tattersalls was formed in 1766, mainly as an auctioneer dealing in horses, and had its first home near Hyde Park in London. Part of the building, the Subscription Rooms, was set aside for members of the

Jockey Club who made use of the facility's privacy to place bets with each other. By 1881, as betting on horse racing became more popular, the Jockey Club recognised the need for a body to resolve disputes and formed the Tattersalls Committee.

But in 1998 Tattersalls Committee could not take over from the Green Seal Service, not least because of the many different types of sporting bets shops had started to accept. In addition, the Tattersalls process was a lengthy one. The committee meet only once a quarter and disputes, although they could be put in writing were, in the main, put to the committee personally.

The betting industry recognised that a new body was required and thus, from the offices of the *Racing Post* at Canary Wharf, and with much assistance from the Trinity Mirror Group and Satellite Information Services (SIS) IBAS was launched in November 1998.

IBAS originally stood for Independent Betting Arbitration Service. But in 2007, in recognition of the fact that IBAS was not an arbitration provider in the legal sense of the word, its name was changed to Independent Betting Adjudication Service in an effort to reflect its true nature.

As with the Green Seal Service, IBAS relies solely on documented evidence. The body does not fight the customer's case, nor does it defend the actions of the bookmaker. It does not try to mediate or broker deals, but simply gives its opinion on bet settlement, based on the bet as captured, together with the bookmaker's operating rules or, where the rules are silent on an issue, best industry practice. The customer's previous betting history is not taken into account.

In 1994 a five-year deal was agreed between bookmakers and the Horserace Betting Levy Board that lead to the funds raised by bookmakers, mainly betting shop owners, rising steadily over the decade. By 1999, the amount donated to the Levy Board was £57million per year.

The method of calculating bookmakers' payments changed too and by the end of the decade was an average of £651 per betting shop plus, on a sliding scale, a percentage of turnover at the rate of 2.5% if turnover reached £310,000 per annum per shop.

CHAPTER EIGHT

INTO THE NEW MILLENNIUM

Betting Levy 10% gross profit, Betting Exchanges-Betfair,
Hillside Girl, Arbing, Hanse Cronje, Internet betting,
Gross Profit Tax, FOBTs, Problem Gambling, Gamcare,
Leaving William Hill, Money Laundering, IBAS, No Smoking,
Turf TV, Virtual Racing, Gambling Commission-Gambling Act,
X-Factor, Kieren Fallon, David Ashforth, Betview and Betting
Business, Barney Curley Sommersturn coup, Turf TV Wafeira,
Chris O'Keeffe, Where we are now summary.

The millennium brought a new dawn but few could have guessed
what radical changes and initiatives lay ahead.

Even the levy changed radically in 2001 when it changed to be based
on betting shop profit and not turnover, reverting partly to what was
in place in 1961 but without provision to pay the levy on a percentage
of turnover if this figure produced more than the percentage on profit.

The percentage on profit scheme immediately sparked a huge
increase in contributions from betting shops. The scheme was set at
10% of gross profit and in the first year it raised £74million and by
the early to mid 2000s it was raising between £90million to well over
£100million per annum. So within 40 years, the amount given to horse
racing by bookmakers had gone from less than £1million in 1961 to
more than £100million per year. Someone was doing something right.
Was it the horse race industry or the betting shops? In recent years
however, with less money bet on horse racing, the amount raised has
steadily dropped and in the year 2010/11 it was £52.77million.

The next radical initiative brings a cold shiver to the spine of
bookmakers: betting exchanges and Betfair in particular.

Launched in June 2000, Betfair emulates what happens in a stock
exchange where a buyer wants to buy shares and a seller wants to sell

them. A bet exchange matches those who want to bet that something will happen with those who want to lay – who say that the same thing will not happen. Thus a market is formed, with money matched by each party at the odds agreed. Anyone wanting to operate a betting exchange must have a bookmaker's licence.

Exchanges can offer punters who betting between themselves better odds than those available from traditional bookmakers. There is, however, a charge that needs to be paid to the exchange, creating its profit, which is paid by the party who wins in the transaction.

Betfair has the lion's share of the betting exchange market, but there are other significant operators in Betdaq and to a lesser extent WBX (World Betting Exchange).

*

Why do traditional bookmakers get hot under the collar at the mention of betting exchanges? One obvious reason is that exchanges pose serious competition – though bookmakers have stood their ground against the Tote, National Lottery and Football Pools. Bookmakers and the horse racing industry have both criticised government and betting exchanges for not contributing their fair share of levies and betting tax. For the exchanges, horserace betting levies and taxes are based on the amount collected in charges from customers who make a profit.

Another widely held concern about exchanges is that they provide a platform for betting that a contender will lose an event – which can lead to skulduggery. Take, for example, an incident in 2003 when the horse Hillside Girl drifted from odds-on to over 20-1 on Betfair. A farrier who had worked for Hillside Girl's stable knew the horse was unsound and had laid her on a betting exchange to a large sum of money. The horse did indeed lose and was pulled up lame.

A further criticism of bet exchanges is that they allow unregulated, unlicensed and untaxed individuals to act as bookmakers. Anyone can log on to a betting exchange website, deposit money and thereafter act as if they are a bookmaker, taking bets on horses (to win or lose). No taxes or betting levies are paid by these individuals, who can choose which bet transactions they want to be involved with. All they have to pay is a percentage of profit made to the exchange.

There is also a belief that some professional organisations have set themselves up as market makers and promoted their markets on betting exchanges. Football markets are one medium in which these organisations thrive, offering customers of exchanges many types of bets. The organisation will set up the market and then seed it – putting liquidity into it.

Betting exchanges have given some the opportunity to class themselves as 'professional' punters, for the sake of ego. But just because a person spends their leisure time studying form and betting does not make them a true professional punter. This title should be reserved for those few individuals who have regularly over years made a living from betting.

The onset of exchanges also provided an opportunity for punters to bet with their hearts rather than their heads. So, on the exchange a Spurs supporter might offer odds of 6-4 against Arsenal beating Spurs, where perhaps the true odds, going by form and players available, and guided by what traditional bookmakers would be offering, would be nearer evens. Thus the shrewd punters, whether Arsenal fans or not, would snap up the 6-4. Value seeking punters, who think they may have found a potential winner, will only strike a bet if the odds on offer were more generous than they should be. So the shrewd professional punter may go days, if not weeks, without placing a bet if he thinks the odds on offer are too tight.

Using a similar example to that of the Spurs fan offering 6-4 that Arsenal will win. An arbitrage (arb) customer will snap up the 6-4, but then place contrary bets on Arsenal not winning and also on the game ending in a draw. With the generous odds of 6-4 against Arsenal and the other bets placed he can ensure that, with all options covered, a profit will be made on any of the three outcomes.

The opportunity to put oneself in a no-lose situation does not come often but, with some research, an early start, a copy of the *Racing Post*, a scan of Pricewise and odds-comparison websites and a look at what is on offer on bet exchanges, situations do present themselves.

One thing that did not change post millennium was betting scandals – which continued to hit the headlines. UK bookmakers were not involved in the first major incident, but it shows how some sportsmen can be bought to lose as well as to win.

In January 2000, South Africa was playing England at cricket, and torrential rain meant a draw was a certainty – but South African Hansie Cronje agreed to a suggestion for each team to forfeit an innings, meaning the game could end in a result.

This was somewhat to the detriment of the South African team, but the cricketing public believed Cronje was acting for the benefit of the game. England won the match in an exciting finish.

In reality, Cronje had received £5,000 and, infamously, a leather jacket from a South African bookmaker who stood to win a large sum should any result other than a draw be achieved. Subsequent investigations revealed Cronje had been involved in many other match fixes.

Two years later the cricketer was killed in an aeroplane crash, which some suspected was not an accident but a means to ensure Cronje could not expose those who lurk in the shadows whenever there is a chance of easy money to be made.

In football, since the reintroduction of fixed-odds coupons, betting had increased hugely in popularity. Bets had been restricted to a minimum of trebles for draws, or fivefolds for any match that contained a home win. The football authorities had enforced these restrictions due to concerns of match fixing, but they were gradually lifted. First for televised live games, then for cup games and finally, in 2002, restrictions were lifted for any game – so it was 'bookmaker beware' if he chose to take bets on minor matches.

Betting was now a global pastime and a source of employment for many. Telephone betting had long been available and many punters worldwide placed bets by phone with UK-based bookmaker, but as people increasingly started to use the internet this soared. Betfair had shown what was possible – the click of a button would produces prices in any event on which there was a betting market. Victor Chandler led the move for some operators to move their whole business to Gibraltar, including telephone and internet betting, in order to avoid tax and levy charges.

Some in the industry stuck their heads in the sand, believing that their punters would have nothing to do with the world-wide web, and continue to tramp down to the betting shop to place their bet. Fearful of change, these operators overlooked the potential worldwide customer base offered by the internet.

At the start there were problems with some websites as the 'dash for cash' culture meant initiatives were put in the public domain before being fully tested. Sites would crash or freeze with punters left wondering whether their bet had been placed. Traders would carefully calculate odds for a market only for them to be transposed incorrectly on to the site by a rushed and harried data transcriber.

Software systems that had not been fully tested were found to be slow or faulty leading to occasions when an event would have started and finished, while on the internet the market would still be on display and bets taken. Few checks or management systems were put in place to ensure these faults were found and corrected.

Chris Bird, head of security at William Hill called me on one such occasion – explaining that our internet site had been subject to a fraud. He wanted us both to go down to Folkestone to speak to police about the matter. On the way we looked at the address of the account holder. It was a nondescript terraced house with, oddly, pieces of furniture stacked in the rear garden. It looked as if the occupants had just moved in and started to dispose of items.

The occupants had been able to gain a relatively large sum from the website because the software accounting system was faulty. Deposits had been made into the account and, because of a glitch, could be withdrawn but would continue to show as a credit in the account.

The account holder had recognised this fault and had taken full advantage of it. We explained this to police who, in turn, interviewed the main suspect. In the meantime, and using a court injunction, the bank account into which the 'winnings' had been paid was frozen. Although the figure was not publicised at the time, John Brown later disclosed that the sum involved was £800,000.

Most of the money or the assets purchased with it was eventually recovered – and the glitch soon remedied. The surprising thing was that the suspect was not a criminal mastermind who had hacked into and breached the systems, but an account holder of average intelligence who had come across a bug. Once bitten twice shy was the lesson and William Hill soon got their act together.

Like it or not, internet betting was here to stay, and because some organisations had moved offshore and were offering customers tax-free betting, it soon affected trade in betting shops. Betting tax was 6.75% and this imposition, plus the betting levy, resulted in deductions of nine pence in the pound.

*

The choice for punters was to bet on the internet from the comfort of their home, or troop down to the betting shop and suffer a deduction of nine pence in the pound. While the betting shop does offer the chance for social engagement and not everyone is comfortable with computers, for many the answer was a no-brainer.

The situation could not continue, and the betting shop industry recognised more lobbying was needed to ensure the government knew the effect it was having on both betting industry and the government's tax revenues. Many operators made noises that they would follow the lead of Chandler and move everything, apart from their bricks-and-mortar business, offshore.

John Brown of William Hill again took the lead and came up with a plan to revolutionise the way betting tax was levied that would, surprisingly, benefit almost all.

Brown said the idea came many years previously from Bob Green of Mecca, was reiterated in 1994 by Will Roseff, an industry leader and proprietor of Backhouse bookmakers, but nothing had come of it at the time.

The idea was for a tax on gross profits rather than turnover: so the greater the profit of the industry the greater the taxes that would be collected. Bookmakers could now take less profitable bets and those from high-rollers and others who bet in large sums but lost little. They would be welcomed back to the legal side of the industry.

It was hoped that illegal betting could even be curtailed as ordinary punters would return to betting shops if there was no tax on stakes. Tax would only be paid by the bookmaker should he make a profit on the bet.

Although the original idea might not have been Brown's it was he who saw the moment to push for it. And despite opposition from some, he persevered and won over the government.

The major operators and the government agreed that any of the large bookmakers who had moved offshore would move back to the UK if Gross Profit Tax (GPT) was introduced; also that the tax would not be passed on to punters who would now be able to bet deduction free.

GPT at 15%, a rate Brown had suggested, was introduced on 1 January 2002, and the betting industry, punters and government are still reaping its benefits today.

Possibly the only industry group that did not welcome GPT was on-course bookmakers. Bets placed at tracks had been tax-free, which gave racecourse layers an advantage. With the opportunities bet exchanges gave its customers and now with punters able to bet tax-free in betting shops, trade started to drop for the traditional course bookmaker.

*

This in turn had a knock-on effect on starting prices returned from the course. Although attendances had held up, due to many promotions and initiatives, the volume of money bet on-course had diminished.

The rows of bookmakers cut prices and margins in an effort to attract bets, which had the knock-on effect of reducing profit margins in the betting shops even lower. It is an issue with which the whole industry is still wrestling.

Before the introduction of GPT, in 1998, a new betting medium had been launched by The Global Draw company – called Fixed Odds Betting Terminals (FOBTs). Steve Frater, formerly of Mecca Bookmakers, in collaboration with an associate who also had an interest in The Global Draw, introduced Random Number Generator (RNG) betting machines into Admiral Bookmakers, a small chain of betting shops they owned.

The machines had the appearance of one-armed bandits, but with a difference. One-armed bandits have a mechanism that ensures they pay out sufficient wins to ensure the percentage payout to the customer, as agreed by the licensing authorities, is maintained. These machines are called compensatory machines and can be found in pubs, clubs and adult gaming centres.

The key aspect of the Fixed Odds Betting Terminal – which made them legal to have in betting shops – was that the random number generator (to determine the winner), was situated outside the premises. In this way, the transaction could be classed as a bet rather than gaming.

Also, the percentage payment to the player is determined by the odds offered within the game played. So, as an example, with a standard roulette wheel (not American wheel which has two zeros),where there is one zero and 36 other numbers, and odds of 35-1 are paid if a winning number is selected, the margin in the favour of the 'house' is approximately 2.75%. Thus, in theory, £97.25 out of every £100 staked is returned to the players.

The winning number is transmitted to the machine via either a satellite link or telephone modem. With later games and legislation which clarified the legal position of these machines, the RNG could be built into the machine, but it still remained independent of the game.

After the introduction of GPT in 2002 the machines were loaded with casino-type roulette games and became known as roulette machines. Before 2002, with tax payable on stakes, although the machines were extremely popular with punters they were not particularly profitable for betting shop operators. The old question of punter 'churn' or 'turnover' which, with tax payable on turnover, remained a constant problem.

A punter could walk into a betting shop with £20 and, because of a constant win/loss throughout the afternoon, place bets with a total value of £100 but still have only the £20 to lose. With FOBT machines where the payback was high at 97.25%, this £20 could be churned so that maybe £500 of stakes could be placed.

*

Hence, at the end of the day, with the customer losing his £20 but with his stakes registered on the machine as £500, at the rate of 6.75% betting tax a sum of £33.75 would need to be paid to the government. This would result in a net loss to the betting shop of £13.75 (£33.75 tax to pay – £20 lost by the punter). So betting shop operators were reluctant to install the machines.

Following the changes brought about on 1 January 2002, FOBTs were an instant success with punters and bookmakers. The betting shop owner did not now care how much churn there was, as tax was now on profit (loss by the punter) and not on stakes.

There are many theories why these machines have become so popular. Some say it is because the payback to the customer is so regular. Indeed, if you want to spend a half hour in a shop and want a good-value bet there is no better than the roulette wheel or other such game where the house has a margin of only 2.75%.

Others say it is the speed of the play that makes the machines so popular. The punter does not have to wait a half an hour for a horse race, neither does he have to wait while the race is run. The bet and the result are instant. If the punter loses he can try again straight away and if he wins he will want to quickly repeat the experience. The punter does not have to spend time studying form, or rely on whether the horse, dog, jockey or player is on form.

Others say it is because the games are simple to understand and easily learnt. Certainly this is the case with roulette. Some others say the popularity is partly due to the machine's anonymity. The punter does not have to write out a bet and hand it to a cashier but can simply load the machine with credit by feeding it notes or coins. The customer can then play until his credit is exhausted or until he wishes to stop and cash in whatever credit balance remains. He does this by pressing a button on the machine, the machine then issues a voucher which can be redeemed at the counter.

Or maybe the reason is simply that the games are fun and attractive to play and provide an escape from humdrum everyday life.

Demand was high for Frater's The Global Draw, along with other gaming machine manufacturers such as Cyberview (which was taken over by Barcrest, who in turn was taken over by Global Draw) and Inspired Gaming. At this point, in the early 2000s ,there were no restrictions on how many machines could be installed in betting shops.

Betting shop operators could not believe what a goldmine the machines were proving. Players were queuing up, and at the end of the day the machines were stuffed with cash. Initially, Frater had as many as 24 machines installed in some of his Admiral shops.

But soon the Department for Culture, Media and Sport and the Gaming Board, along with casino operators, were taking a keen interest. Some believed the machine was casino-type 'gaming' and were taking trade away from casinos and adult gaming centres (AGCs). The betting industry, via the ABB, believed what was on offer were bets.

*

In the early 2000s, in an effort to head off adverse action against FOBTs in betting shops, the ABB drew up a code of conduct for their supply and use. This included the restriction of only four machines being allowed per betting shop and restrictions on the maximum stake and payouts.

By this time BOLA had merged with the organisation that represented the interests of the smaller independent betting shops, the BBOA. Warwick Bartlett, who had previously headed the BBOA, became ABB chairman.

The following year the regulatory authority used most of what was contained in the ABB code of conduct as the framework for their controls on the supply and use of gaming machines. In addition, independent testing houses were sourced, inspected and licensed by the regulator. These were tasked to ensure that the games installed on the machines were fair and that the random number generator used were truly random.

It is proper and correct that these regulatory disciplines were put in place, not least because players question the integrity of the random number generator and the independence of the game and machine supplier.

Disgruntled players often believed that the random number generator was not random and that the winning number was selected only because it was the one with fewest bets. Other punters could be heard accusing betting shop staff of tampering with the machine via electronic switches behind the counter.

To be blunt, there was no need for the machines to be fixed. Why would any betting shop owner, machine manufacturer, game supplier, testing-house owner or random number generator want to do anything underhand to machines which bring such regular profit and which have brought a lifeline to the industry?

For those in horse racing, the introduction of gaming machines into betting shops was a move in the wrong direction. Diehards of the horse racing industry cannot perceive how a large portion of betting shop customers have turned their back on the Sport of Kings and instead chosen to spend their cash on machines.

Maybe it is a little surprising when one considers the excitement of the Grand National and Cheltenham Festival, the glamour of Royal Ascot, the romance of the Derby or the wonder of Glorious Goodwood.

There is also the pure fun of a sunny evening meeting at Windsor, or a last-minute and unplanned visit to a mid-week meeting at Lingfield.

But although racecourse attendance is holding up, even increasing for some events, the public search out other betting opportunities and who are we to criticise them for it? Look in most betting shops and you will see a group gathered around the machines, either watching the action or waiting for their turn to play. There will be racing on the large-screen televisions, the audio broadcast will be relaying commentaries, the staff will be at the counter waiting to process any bets offered, but most of the customers will have their back on all this and instead be engrossed in the machines. More and more punters are literally turning their backs on the horse racing product.

*

Around 40% of betting shop profit is produced from the terminals. If it were not for the gaming machines at least a third of the UK's 8,500 betting shops in 2011 would be unviable. Some put the reliance on these terminals by betting shops at a much higher figure.

Assuming the punters who use the machines would not turn back to betting on horse racing, if gaming machines were banned, around 10,000 jobs would be lost in the betting shop industry if some 3000 or so betting shops closed. Plus the jobs lost in the manufacturing and supply of the machines.

This betting medium does not come without issues – such as extra work for betting shop staff and being a magnet for robbers. In the early days when machine cabinets were quite flimsy, it was not unusual to hear of a gang descending on a shop, crowbars at the ready, and within an instant the front of the machine would be jemmied open and the cash box stolen.

Then there was the problem of making payment to those who held winning receipts, issued by the gaming machine. Remembering that the cash used to produce the voucher was locked away in the machine. This dilemma has been partly solved by encouraging players to deposit money at the counter, and then counter staff can remotely load the machine with credit. This goes some way to solving the time-consuming task of counting and checking the cash in the machine at close of business.

The main issue, however, is the suggestion that the machines encourage a propensity for problem gambling. Some have darkly called the terminals the crack cocaine of gambling on the high street. The blame for problem gambling has been laid at the doors of racing, card playing, casinos, football pools, bingo, the National Lottery and now gaming machines. And there is no reason to think that the removal of gaming machines from betting shops would solve the difficulties of those who have an addiction to gambling.

There is help at hand for any addict who wishes to accept it. The organisation GamCare was formed in 2007 by Paul Bellringer OBE after he realised the extent and consequences of problem gambling while working in the probation service. Recognising that there were few facilities for those with gambling dependency and with no cohesive national approach on the issue he set about creating the charity. He used force of personality to encourage the hard-nosed chief executives of the betting industry to donate to the cause. Some of these chief executives are not as cold-blooded as they make themselves out to be and they saw the sense of what Bellringer was trying to achieve.

GamCare is now funded by the GREaT (Gambling Research Education and Treatment) Foundation, which in turn gets its backing from betting and gaming companies and aims to raise £5million a year. This it uses to fund education, treatment and research initiatives that tackle problem gambling and promote responsible gambling. Some may be surprised to learn that the £5million is given voluntarily by the betting industry – a tribute to bookmakers and to the efforts of the GREaT Foundation and its chief executive, Geoffrey Godbold OBE.

GamCare provides practical and emotional help to those who suffer from addiction through support by telephone and online and by providing one-to-one counselling.

Bellringer was instrumental in working with Ladbrokes to devise a voluntary code of responsible gambling that was readily endorsed and recommended by the ABB. That code forms the foundation of the responsible gambling requirements in the Licence Conditions and Code of Practice contained in the 2005 Gambling Act. One aspect of this code is that of self-exclusion. Simple but effective, if a gambler recognises they have a problem they can sign an agreement which bans them from a particular betting office or offices for a defined period.

Cynics said very few people would self-exclude, but statistics show that the numbers opting for this increases year-on-year. In 2009/2010 16,107 customers self-excluded. Although some may renege on the agreement and seek alternative means to place bets, the majority use it as a first step to addressing their gambling behaviour.

The process of self-exclusion from a betting shop involves the punter giving their photograph to the bookmaker and signing a declaration that no bets should be accepted from him. The agreement normally lasts for at least six months.

Unsurprisingly a few scallywags try to take advantage of the process. A person will go through the self-exclusion process and then, by means of a little subterfuge, places bets. If the bets are successful the winnings are collected, if the bets lose the person declares he is self-excluded and demands the return of the stakes.

An incident that touches on the abuse of a sensible measure was that of a gambler who placed £347,000 on America to win the 2006 Ryder Cup. At the time it was the largest golf bet in history and would have returned £753,000 if successful. The bet lost and the punter said he realised his betting was getting out of hand. He asked William Hill to close his telephone account as he wanted to be self-excluded.

The account was closed, but after a short while the punter claimed he had opened another telephone account to place bets with and had also placed large cash bets in William Hill shops. He said that in total he had lost just under £2.1 million while being self-excluded. He then took William Hill to the High Court, claiming the bookmaker had a duty of care towards him and that he should not have been allowed to lose the £2.1million while excluded.

This was a test case and betting shop owners up and down Britain feared that if the punter was successful it would open the floodgates to similar action. But the judge ruled that William Hill owed no duty of care to the punter and that his pathological gambling would still probably have led him to financial ruin, but maybe over a longer period. The industry breathed a sigh of relief.

It was about this time that, after more than 30 years with William Hill, I decided it was time to move on. My responsibilities as regional security manager were changing – for example the task of auditing shops business was transferred away from my department to a new one in Leeds. I was given the choice of staying on in London and taking on other security responsibilities, or of leaving and receiving a more than generous exit package. It took little longer than five minutes for me to agree to the exit package. My bank manager was very pleased.

The exodus to Leeds of the auditing responsibility, and some other tasks, would take several months and I stayed on to oversee a smooth transition of the process. This gave me a year to plan – either for retirement or something new in perhaps a part-time or self-employed working life, or a mix of all.

I formed a consultancy company whose main service was giving independent expert-witness advice to the law enforcement agencies and judiciary in relation to betting and money laundering. I was accepted as a member of the Expert Witness Institute.

Money laundering and the Proceeds of Crime Act 2002 were growing subjects in betting. William Hill's head of security Chris Bird had warned staff of the perils of knowingly accepting bets from anyone suspected of being involved in crime. If they did accept such bets they would be committing a criminal act by aiding the actions of money launderers. I was part of the communication chain to which betting shop staff could report their suspicions. Thereafter advice could be given and the correct course of action taken.

It was a tricky subject and often a difficult call. As an example, should the likes of Terry Ramsden, or the golf punter who came into shops with bags full of cash, be suspected of using the proceeds of crime and their activities passed on to the authorities?

Betting companies now take the matter of money laundering seriously and have designated reporting officers. Before his well-earned retirement, Ladbrokes employed Peter Brewin, an expert in his field who has given me plenty of good advice on money-laundering legislation over the years. Coral has Peter Meacock, Ladbrokes has Chris Cyronni and, following the retirement of Chris Bird, William Hill now have Bill South to oversee any money laundering issues.

Some companies were initially oblivious to the specific requirements of the money laundering legislation and thought it did not apply to them. However, by a process of education, most bookmakers now recognise the need for legal compliance and to have relevant procedures in place to detect potential offences.

For any bookmakers who have yet to be enlightened I would suggest they get their act together before a police officer knocks on their door and asks about a punter who has lost £50,000 over six months and has been arrested for drug dealing; or about a solicitor who has lost a large amount and subsequently been arrested for stealing clients' funds.

*

The first questions the officer will ask the betting shop owner are: 'Have you not got a KYC (know your customer) policy? Were you not suspicious about this young guy who was driving a BMW, dressed in designer clothes, covered in bling, yet never went to work and was betting and often losing £250 or more per race?' Maybe these examples are too obvious, but you no doubt get the drift.

Certainly some of the cases I have dealt with in my consultancy left the bookmakers involved with egg on their faces.

My first case concerned a bookmaker from Northern Ireland. Officers from the Police Service of Northern Ireland (PSNI), which was formerly known as the RUC (Royal Ulster Constabulary) had contacted me with suspicions that an on-course bookmaker was assisting a criminal to launder money. It appeared that the bookmaker was issuing his company cheques to the criminal in exchange for the same cash value plus a fee. Money launderers do not mind taking a 'hit' on their money in order to make it 'clean'. The object was to make it appear that the criminal had won his ill-gotten gains from betting.

For security, the officers felt it prudent to visit me in England to discuss the case and to show me the exhibits and evidence that they had compiled. They came to my home, and I was puzzled to watch the two officers approach my house separately and from different directions. Possibly fearing the answer, I didn't ask why. We had an enjoyable evening after the case was discussed, and it felt somewhat surreal having police officers in my house, discussing the troubles and criminal activity in Northern Ireland, while eating beef bourguignon and quaffing red wine.

A year or so later the case came to court and the judge found the suspects guilty, handing out heavy fines and prison sentences. Interestingly, cases involving suspected terrorist defendants are heard by a judge alone, there are no juries for these type of cases in Northern Ireland. Many subsequent cases from Northern Ireland have since come my way due to the help that I was able to give the officers and the court in this particular case.

Another case involved a pair from Liverpool, neither of whom had done a day of salaried, taxable work in their lives. One of their sources of income was ticket touting, but it was suspected they were involved in other scams, including illegal bookmaking.

When arrested, large bundles of cash was found at their homes and they told police that they were both professional gamblers. Their story was all smoke and mirrors, with tales of winning accounts with betting exchanges, winning from friends and acquaintances and from betting shops throughout Liverpool.

The police in charge of the case were having difficulty understanding the betting terminology and the tales that the pair put forward. Laying and backing on the betting exchanges, taking bets but laying them off in betting shops, then supposedly finding better odds backing the selections on the exchanges – it sent the officers' heads into a spin.

So I was invited to join research on the pair's betting history. With my assistance and subsequent testimony in court, the prosecution was able to discredit their assertions that they were shrewd, professional gamblers. They were both found guilty of money laundering.

Soon after leaving William Hill I took the opportunity of joining the Independent Betting Adjudication Service Ltd (IBAS). I had previously met its chief executive Chris O'Keeffe and found his enthusiasm and commitment to the organisation infectious. And although I had my consultancy business to nurture, IBAS gave me a good opportunity to remain involved with the betting industry.

O'Keeffe explained that IBAS has a panel of betting experts who decide how a dispute should be settled. There is an administration office back-up team who deal with the day-to-day issues and handle the many telephone calls from irate punters claiming to have been unfairly treated by the bookmaker. IBAS also deals with disputes involving betting exchanges, adult gaming centres and other betting mediums.

The IBAS panel consists of a mixture of sports journalists, those who have retired from the betting industry and others with a wealth of experience, senior civil servants who have a law background and have been involved with the betting and gaming industry during their career.

An article I wrote for the IBAS annual report of 2006 headed 'The view from the case manager's office' may give an insight into the issues the body has to deal with and reflect some of the disputes betting shops have to confront.

Nowadays IBAS issues well over 2,000 rulings on bet disputes each year so those summarised in the following article are therefore just a small sample.

THE VIEW FROM THE CASE MANAGER'S OFFICE 2006
JANUARY
Formula 1 racing

The New Year started with a dispute that had been carried over from 2005. This involved the US Formula One Grand Prix.

Some bookmakers and their customers were in dispute due to a large number of F1 drivers who were using Michelin tyres, refusing to continue in the US Grand Prix, following the opening 'introductory' lap. Only six drivers, who were not using Michelin tyres, continued the race and eventually Michael Schumacher crossed the finishing line first.

Some punters, who it appears were privy to inside information regarding tyre safety, recognised that there would be many drivers who, although completing the 'introductory lap', would refuse to compete in the race. So these punters correctly judged that Schumacher, who was not using Michelin tyres, would indeed go on to complete the course and have a great chance of victory at an inflated price. It could therefore have been perceived that a number of the fancied Michelin drivers would, due to non-participation, receive a DNF (did not finish) classification – a popular bet particularly with online punters.

Many bookmakers had a rule to cover this eventuality, which stated that the start of the formation lap was indeed the start of the race. Others did not. The official rules of the FIA (Federation Internationale de L'Automobile) made it clear that the start of the race occurs only after all the cars have returned to the grid after the formation lap and the starting procedure is executed.

Some bookmakers had no provision in their rules for such an eventuality. It was left to IBAS to rule on what circumstances constituted the actual start of an FI race; the main claim from punters being that money should be refunded to those who had placed bets on the drivers that did not carry on in the race, after the 'introductory' lap.

The IBAS panel ruled in line with the bookmaker's rules. But if the bookmaker had no specific rule in place then the competition rules were applied.

FEBRUARY
Wembley Stadium

The building of the new Wembley Stadium caused controversy when some bookmakers' customers approached IBAS as their bets on whether or not the stadium would be built in time for the 2006 FA Cup were delayed in being paid.

It may have been coincidental but the majority of these customers were based in the Wembley and surrounding areas and declared that they actually worked on the Wembley stadium site! Before the matter escalated to a formal panel ruling the bookmakers conceded and all bets were paid.

MARCH
Racecourse judges

Errors made by racecourse judges were a topic of conversation and dispute on more than one occasion during March. The 4.30pm Lingfield on 6 March was a case in point where the judge called the wrong result in a photo-finish. The judge noticed her mistake but only after the 'weighed in' announcement was made – rendering it too late to make any difference to payments made by the Tote and many bookmakers.

The Cheltenham Festival was soon upon us and, in the main, resulted in few betting disputes; though one betting market that did cause controversy involved the leading trainer prize.

The judges initially awarded the title to Nicky Henderson and consequently bookmakers paid out on this result. Some bookmakers, however, recognised that a mistake had been made and paid winning bets out on Paul Nicholls.

It was belatedly decided by the judges that the winner should indeed have been Nicholls, who had the same number of Cheltenham winners as Henderson but won the trainers' title by gaining more prize money.

The whole episode left bookmakers and customers in doubt as to the correct way to settle winning-trainer bets and some punters were left disappointed that they again were out of pocket following a judge's initial incorrect decision and the subsequent (later proved to be erroneous) Press Association announcement. IBAS ruled that bets should be settled on the original announcement.

In the panel's view the practice of using the result on the day, or at the weighed-in, for betting purposes has stood the test of time and most punters appreciate the fact that they are as likely to win as lose through this application.

All in all March was not a good month for racecourse judges or punters who rely on accurate decisions.

Tipping service

The month ended with IBAS helping to give some common sense guidance to a man who had contacted the office with a tale of woe. He stated he had given £2,000 to a man who had presented himself as a racehorse tipster. Not surprisingly, once the £2,000 was paid over, the 'tipster' was not heard from again.

Although outside the remit of IBAS, we advised the man who had paid the £2,000 to contact his local Trading Standards office and the police – courses of action that had not occurred to him. The following day the man rang to thank IBAS for the advice and to inform us that the Fraud Squad had visited him and was taking a keen interest in the matter.

The next day the sorry tale was reported in the *Racing Post*, forewarning others of this con. We live in hope that the police are able to track down and prosecute the con man and that the £2,000 will be recovered.

APRIL
Grand National

The Grand National, not for the first time, had a false start. Fortunately, officials were on the ball this time and were able to halt the horses after they had run just a few yards. The restart was not unduly delayed and eventually the 2006 Grand National was under way.

One dispute of note arising from the National was where one bookmaker had cause to rue the inefficiency of his screen display system when a price of 16-1 was shown for there being no more than nine fallers in the big race. Many clients took advantage of these displayed odds only to find that the actual odds referred to there being no more than nine fallers 'at the first fence'.

It is an established principle in betting that where there may be doubt over a proposition then the price is used to determine the bet. In this case the bookmaker stated the prices were displayed as being for the first fence in the Grand National but the customers claimed there was no mention of the first fence. It was impossible for the panel to give an opinion on what was displayed but the odds would make no sense if applied to the whole race rather than the first fence.

Man brought back to life?

The remainder of April was relatively quiet but a dispute over whether a man could be brought back to life after being dead for 24 hours brought a macabre, yet humorous, note to proceedings.

A bookmaker had laid a client 1,000-1 that this would not happen before the year 2014. Soon after the bet was laid it was announced in a tabloid that this had indeed happened in Japan, but the customer complained that the bookmaker was refusing to pay out. Subsequent enquiries revealed that the man who had been 'brought back to life' was a Japanese soldier who had been 'missing presumed dead' since the Second World War.

It was a lesson to always clarify the conditions before a bet is struck. Although the bet was not successful for the customer on this occasion, he does have a few more years remaining before his bet is definitely a losing one!

MAY

John Prescott

The political arena was the subject of discussions at IBAS when a customer reported that a bet he had placed on John Prescott losing his job was not paid by the bookmaker. Indeed many people in the country were left wondering what Prescott was actually doing to still retain his Deputy Prime Minister title, salary and associated perks, considering that a large part of his responsibilities had been transferred to other ministers. This followed newspaper revelations of an affair Prescott had with his Diary Secretary.

While the Panel agreed with the customer that the bet could have been more clearly defined, they did not agree that Prescott had lost his job, despite being stripped of his roles as Secretary of State for Local Government and the Regions. He may no longer be performing that role but still held the office of Deputy Prime Minister and received a salary for that position. The panel therefore concluded that Prescott's job had changed but not ceased.

FA Cup

Football disputes continued to form a major part of the IBAS postbag during May. The FA Cup final, played between West Ham and Liverpool, started with a Liverpool own goal and after normal time the score was 3-3. Liverpool won the game at the end of extra time.

An own goal and a draw after 90 minutes is a recipe for disputes and this match was no exception. Customers with bets on the own goal scorer being their 'first goal scorer' believed they should be paid, others believed that injury time should not count towards the 'normal 90 minutes play' and that the clock should stop dead on 90 minutes, therefore making their bets on Liverpool to win at the end of 'normal time' winning ones.

Others had taken odds of around 8-13 for Liverpool to win at the end of normal time, rather than for Liverpool to win the cup outright, which were around 1-4. These customers were peeved to discover their bets, that simply stated 'Liverpool to win' at odds of 8-13, were losers.

Dodgy lasagna hits football team

Still with football (and West Ham) the Marriott Hotel in Docklands was at the centre of intrigue when ten of the Spurs players went down with a mysterious stomach bug a few hours before their game with West Ham. The intrigue deepened when it was reported that high rollers on betting sites based in the Far East had wagered substantial money on West Ham to win the match (which they eventually did).

A 'dodgy' lasagna was initially believed to be the cause of the stomach upset and some conspiracy theorists wondered if the meal had been tampered with. It could possibly just have been 'pasta' its sell-by date.

Eventually the lasagna was cleared of blame and a virus that had spread among the team was found to be the problem. Someone near to the team and/or hotel may have discovered early on the day of the game that the Spurs squad had a problem and took advantage in the betting world.

JUNE

The Derby and Royal Ascot came and went without too much controversy.

The 90-minute football rule

June also saw the start of the World Cup. Predictably the 90-minute rule, whereby all football bets are settled on the result at the end of normal (90 minutes) play, with there being three possible outcomes to the match (ie home win, away win and draw), was the source of many disputes.

Consequently those having bets on a team to win, but that team winning only in extra time, were disappointed to find that their bets were losers unless they had stipulated "outright win" or "to go through to the next round" or similar on their bet.

Surprisingly, there were still some customers, who having placed bets on the basis of normal time (90 minutes of play), were still expecting their wagers to be winners when their bet was winning at the stroke of a TV clock showing the game had been on for 90 minutes. In fact, due to injury time, the referee had not blown his whistle for the end of normal time. Subsequently, with a goal or goals being scored in injury time, causing a selected team not to win, many customers felt aggrieved that their bookmaker would not pay out.

JULY
World Cup coupons

By the time the end of the World Cup was in sight (9 July) there had been one major dispute of note. This centered on a bookmaker distributing World Cup coupons with a price error, and many customers snapping up the odds of 3-1 for a treble that was advertised on the coupon, whereas odds of 2-1 should have been on offer.

Some could say the bookmaker palpable error rule would cover this eventuality but others might say it would not be obvious to many that a price of 3-1 should be 2-1.

After some deliberation the bookmaker made a discretionary payment at 3-1 to those clients who had approached IBAS.

AUGUST
Cricket ball tampering

The fourth Test match between England and Pakistan brought betting controversy when officials decided Pakistan had forfeited the match by refusing to return to the field after tea on day four at the Brit Oval. This followed the umpire awarding five penalty runs to England due to an allegation of ball tampering by Pakistan.

At the time Pakistan had been playing well and were set to win the match. To the annoyance of punters who had backed Pakistan and had been expecting to be on a winning bet, bookmakers paid on the 'official' result of an England win.

At least one bookmaker, in the interests of customer service, went further and, at a stated additional cost of £15,000, returned stakes on 'losing' bets involving Pakistan to win and on the draw.

While the panel recognised the disappointment of punters who backed Pakistan or the draw, the panel could only confirm that the industry had settled the disputed bets correctly as losers as an official result was declared.

SEPTEMBER
Football manager appointment

Roy Keane's appointment as manager of Sunderland brought belated claims from customers who had earlier in the year backed him to be the next manager of the club. In the interim however – during July – Niall Quinn, the Sunderland chairman, had appointed himself as manager.

Some would say that the subsequent appointment of Keane indicated that Quinn's appointment was only temporary and that bets placed before July for Keane to be appointed as 'next manager' should be classed as winners, in other words ignoring that Quinn had been appointed in the interim.

As a gesture of goodwill a few bookmakers paid on both

results. But, for those who had already paid out to punters who with money on Quinn, it was difficult to see how they should be forced to make payment again to those who had bet on Keane. Consequently, the panel supported those bookmakers and betting exchanges that had paid out on Quinn, as Sunderland FC had in a statement 'officially' confirmed his appointment.

Golf sportsmanship called into question

The Ryder Cup was not without controversy. During play on the last day of the tournament, with many players still out on the course but with the Cup already won by Europe, one member of the European team, on his 18th hole, graciously conceded a long putt to his American opponent which resulted in their match being halved.

Many punters complained this had denied them winning bets involving the size of Europe's win margin and bets on the winner of this match. A media representative of one of the larger bookmakers was quoted as saying 'sporting events are not put on for the benefit of the betting public' thus it could be said that betting fortune comes with the rub of the green.

The panel's ruling pointed out that although appreciating that the European player would not have conceded the putt if the Ryder Cup had been in the balance, it did not alter the fact that the official result was that the match was halved. The bookmaker's rules left them with no option but to settle on that official result.

Mistaken SP

September continued to be a month of unusual controversies when a greyhound SP, returned from a race at an evening meeting at Kinsley stadium, was put under the spotlight.

The SP for the winner was originally listed on the Kinsley stadium website as 5-2 favourite, with the other five dogs all being returned at 3-1. On the morning following the race it was reported that 'out of the ordinary' bets had been placed in betting shops on the unnamed returned favourite for the race.

Following an investigation and an inspection of the on-course bookmakers' ledgers, the reporter whose job it was to declare the official SP accepted he had made a mistake in returning it. So on the day that the Racing Post was due to publish the race results, it was calculated that the winner should, and indeed was, returned as 7-2 and not the favourite.

OCTOBER
Bookmaker suspended from IBAS register

October saw the culmination of an issue that had been running for weeks, during which several phone calls had been received from customers of one specialist sports internet bookmaker. They were complaining of late payment and non-payment of winnings and deposited money.

Attempts by IBAS to resolve the issue were met with no response from the bookmaker, so the decision was taken to suspend the bookmaker from its register.

Over the next few days reporters from the sporting press picked up on the story and the issue was soon concluded when the bookmaker announced on his website that he had ceased trading.

NOVEMBER
Bookmaker limit causes controversy

November brought a dispute from a client who, despite winning over £244,750 for a stake of £42, was unhappy that more cash was not forthcoming.

His point was that his multiple each-way bet had money running on to a selection that, should it have won, would have hit the bookmaker's limit and thus the full winnings would not have been paid. Hence he was claiming that he was due a large part of this running-on money.

Although an interesting point, the panel disagreed with the notion that money built up from winners in a multiple bet and then lost on one of the multiple bet selections should be refunded.

DECEMBER
Allegations of match fixing at snooker tournament
The year ended with accusations of match rigging during the first round of the Snooker UK Championship. Various Irish-based bookmakers refused to pay out on a snooker match which, they claimed, had been the subject of an abnormally large number of correct-frame win bets.

So they had voided all bets on this particular match under their match rigging rules. Although there was disappointment from punters who had placed these bets, equally there was joy from other punters who had placed losing bets on the match.

The decision to void all bets was thus welcomed by punters who had placed losing bets, including one who asked not to be named because he did not want his wife to know how much he had staked. He said: "I had €2,000 on the loser and was gutted when I saw he had lost. Fair play to the bookmaker for returning stakes, although if they are not paying out on winning bets it must be the right thing to do."

Thus ended yet another interesting year; no doubt 2007 will bring as many, if not more, diverse betting incidents

*

The design of betting shops continued to improve over the years, with the provision of disabled access, hearing loops, air conditioning, refreshment areas, no-smoking areas, carpets and customer toilets (male, female and disabled) becoming standard for newly fitted shops. Thus the no-smoking legislation which came into force on 1 July 2007 was not completely alien to some betting shop environments. The media reported loss of trade from such places as bingo clubs, but betting shops were not so badly affected.

Any punter wishing to smoke could walk a few paces to the front door, have a cigarette and quickly return to the fray. Staff were glad of the fresh air at work and in the main it was a piece of legislation the betting industry welcomed.

*

A further question for betting shop proprietors was whether to take Turf TV pictures. Launched in April 2007, Turf TV challenged the monopoly SIS had enjoyed for over 20 years in supplying live racing footage to betting shops. The firm had been busily signing up racecourses to an agreement giving Turf TV sole rights to broadcast live pictures from each track into betting shops. By the time of its launch, Turf TV had five racecourses signed up and within a year it had 31 on board. These racecourses included such high-profile tracks as Aintree, Ascot, Cheltenham, Chester, Goodwood, Newbury, Newmarket and York. Imagine betting shop owners and punters, relying only on the SIS service and being deprived of pictures of the Grand National, Royal Ascot, Cheltenham Festival, Glorious Goodwood and the like.

At first the major bookmakers refused to take Turf TV, no doubt hoping that if starved of a cash flow it would soon fold. But the smaller independents saw a potential gap in the market for themselves and signed up to both SIS and Turf TV, allowing their customers to view racing from every racecourse in Britain. If racing was taking place only at Turf TV courses, there were no live pictures in the larger companies' shops.

The large organisations initially held firm and brought legal action on the grounds that Turf TV had acted incorrectly in its negotiations with the racecourses. This action was protracted and expensive for all concerned and eventually proved unsuccessful. The major bookmakers don't lose many battles, but this one was the exception.

Their ranks collapsed as their customers started to vote with their feet and trade began to suffer. The Tote and Coral were the first to give in, closely followed by Ladbrokes and Hills in January 2008. Betfred was the last major player to hold out, but they finally relented in April 2009.

The only bookmaker who still refuses to sign up to Turf TV is Chisholm. Howard Chisholm, a major influence in the betting shop industry, believes his business can get along without the expense. Chisholm has long stated that, in his shops at least, the cost of the horse racing product is too high and out of proportion with the turnover it attracts.

*

Meanwhile, SIS and Turf TV are learning to live with each other. In December 2010, with snow ravaging the horse-racing calendar, the two firms cooperated to broadcast a meeting from Mauritius into UK and Irish betting shops. Maybe this is the shape of things to come?

The expense of Turf TV was, and still is, used by the betting industry as a bargaining tool when subsequent horserace betting levy schemes were discussed. They explained that racing turnover was decreasing yet the cost of bringing horse racing to the betting public was increasing. And this increase in costs was going not only into the pockets of Turf TV but also to horse racing itself. Turf TV was paying rights charges to the racecourses that allowed it to broadcast pictures.

At a rate of around £6,000 per shop, and with 8,500 betting shops (though not all were taking the Turf TV service), Turf TV could be estimated to be collecting in the region of £50million per year from the betting industry. Some argued that this was an additional expense that, if Turf TV were not in business, would not need to be paid. Others made the point that a large part of this money was going straight to the 31 racecourses who had signed up to Turf TV, and thus to the horse racing industry. So, in the last few years, with the levy raising sums of between £85million and £90million (£75.4million in 2009/10), compared to just over £100million in the years before Turf TV, the betting shop industry considered it was paying more than enough – and some said far too much – to the horse racing industry.

This was on top of the fact that betting shop punters were continuing to turn to gaming machines over horse racing – which in recent years has dipped below 50% of shop turnover.

Virtual racing events were introduced by the 49s organisation to fill in the gaps between real races – and when there was disruption to the scheduled racing programme.

Who would have thought in 1961 that, some 45 years later, punters in betting shops would be buying a packet of crisps or chocolate bar with a cup of coffee before sitting down comfortably to watch what some describe as cartoon race events on large TV screens; not only watch but actually bet money on them. The outcome of these events is determined by a random number generator and the pictures of the 'race', as with any virtual-reality event, are simply cosmetic and displayed for visual effect. It has long been said that most punters will bet on anything, including two flies climbing up a wall, and it looks like whoever coined the aphorism was correct.

Rumoured plans to expand the virtual product gathered credence at the 2010 ICE Totally Gaming show when SIS and Inspired Gaming announced they launching a virtual-betting channel for betting shops and international subscribers. The virtual content of the channel would include football, horse and greyhound racing, motor racing, speedway, roulette, lotto and cycling. It is envisaged that there will be more than 100 real-time events scheduled each day at five-minute intervals. The quality of the virtual product is now being described by some as 'blurring the distinction between what is live and what is virtual'. Maybe Chisholm and some other betting shop operators are right when they say, who needs the real horse racing product?

Radical thoughts by Chisolm, but we were now in radical times. The Gambling Act 2005 was introduced on 1 September 2007, along with the Gambling Commission – the government body responsible for the Act's regulation and enforcement. The Act aimed to keep crime out of betting, protect the weak and vulnerable (particularly those under the age of 18), and ensure that betting was fair and open. Another major provision was the demise of the demand test: the need to prove, to the satisfaction of the local licensing magistrates, that there was a demand for a new betting shop.

Although police and local councils could still make objections to protect the vulnerable (no betting shops opening next to a school for instance) it became open house. The government, determined that the free market would drive the economy forward, hoped that financial viability would determine the survival of a new shop.

Gambling transactions could now be treated as contracts under the Act, allowing both bet disputes and non-payments to be taken to court. Betting was no longer a matter of honour. One other provision of the Act was the power given to the Gambling Commission (the Commission) to make a bet void should it believe the contract that the bet represented was substantially unfair.

The industry had to wait until April 2011 before the Commission felt it necessary to use its power to void a bet. The press release, dated 7 April 2011, concerning the case read:

> The Gambling Commission has today concluded an investigation into suspicious betting patterns involving employees of Virgin Media and has decided to void bets totaling over £16,000 placed on TV's the X Factor. The voiding orders, the first of their kind under the Gambling Act 2005, follow a Commission investigation into a report of suspicious betting activity brought to our attention by Betfair's Integrity Unit. No other major betting operators were involved.
>
> The investigation established that individuals employed by phone line operator Virgin Media were misusing their access to Virgin's data on voting patterns to place unfair bets on which contestants would be eliminated from the X Factor. There is no evidence that the integrity of the public voting, or the TV shows involved, were compromised. However, the Commission

has consulted with Ofcom, which has been working with Virgin Media and other relevant stakeholders, to ensure that firm steps are taken to prevent a repeat of such activity.

Commenting on the case, the Gambling Commission's Director of Regulation, Nick Tofiluk said:

"Following a multi-agency investigation led by the Gambling Commission, we are satisfied that the bets placed were substantially unfair as the individuals involved had inside information. We have worked closely with all the bodies involved to ensure that those individuals do not profit from their activity and that appropriate action has been taken to prevent a recurrence of such activity in the future."

The local council still issues the betting office licence, but it is to the Gambling Commission that would-be bookmakers must turn in order to apply for their company operating licence and personal betting licence.

The cost of running the Commission – with its offices, inspector and administrative backup – is approximately £6million per year and this is raised via annual fees charged to bookmakers for their licences. Betting shop owners have been constant critics of the Commission and maintain that they were already a well regulated and licensed industry and that there was no need for further expensive regulation.

*

At the end of 2007, the trail at the Old Bailey of Kieren Fallon and five others accused of corruption collapsed after two months when the judge, Mr Justice Forbes, instructed the jury to acquit the defendants on the grounds that a lack of evidence meant there was no case to answer.

The actual case began to fall apart when an expert witness from New South Wales was brought to the witness stand by the prosecution to view the videos of the races involved and to give an opinion on what he saw. The case had already been running for many weeks and had cost over £6million to stage. A barrister for the defense asked the expert witness a pivotal question about his qualifications, to which the witness responded: "I haven't said I am an expert in UK racing".

A bombshell had hit the court. The judge said he found it remarkable how long it had taken for the expert's limitations to become known. Concluding that the witness's evidence had been discredited, the judge directed the jury to return not guilty verdicts on all the defendants.

I don't know how stringent the courts are in Australia, but certainly in the UK an expert witness will be challenged in court on his credentials for the case to be heard. I have been in this position many times, as have all expert witnesses. One would have thought this witness would have anticipated such a question and would have told the CPS, long before the case was heard, how he would answer.

The trial was covered by the world's media, but among the most respected coverage was that by the seasoned David Ashforth, a journalist with a particular affinity for covering the world of bookmaking and betting shops. As with other great journalists, when the reader sees Ashforth's byline they know they have a treat in store. Informative, humourous and filled with integrity and knowledge, Ashforth's pieces entertained readers of *The Sporting Life,* which he joined in 1990, and subsequently the *Racing Post* until his retirement at the end of 2010.

In 2008, Ashforth's peers in the Horserace Writers and Photographers Association voted him Journalist of the Year, with his coverage of the Fallon trail earning a major contribution of the votes.

*

Under the Gambling Act the only day a betting shop cannot open is Christmas Day, meaning shops were open for the first Good Friday on 21 March 2008. Although there was no horse racing in Britain there was in Europe and South Africa as well as greyhound racing and the ever-present gaming machines for punters to bet on.

By now betting shop staff had fully realised, and accepted, that they had to work unsocial hours. But their efforts do not go unnoticed and, apart from any employer incentives and rewards, the *Racing Post* and SIS give a Betting Shop Manager of the Year award. Mystery shoppers visit the nominees, and a subsequent shortlist is interviewed by a panel of industry experts including Brough Scott and Jim Cremin from the *Racing Post*. The main qualities sought are product knowledge and customer service.

The finals are held at a lunch in a five-star West End hotel and the main prize is a luxury trip to Dubai. It is not unusual for the Manager of the Year to also be rewarded by their employer something that has, on several occasions in the past, been a car or its equivalent.

In 2007 the Sky media company launched the monthly magazine Betview to be distributed free of charge across the betting industry. Sky recognised that general sports betting, and not just horse racing, would play a major part in the future of betting shops. Football betting had taken off in particular, a sport with which Sky has a major influence. The company already produced a magazine called *Preview* promoting the Sky Sports channels, which was distributed to pubs.

*

In addition to many interesting articles, *Betview* carries a full TV listing schedule showing upcoming sporting events that will be broadcast into betting shops. The magazine has introduced its own annual awards for those in the betting industry and again nominees are visited by a mystery shopper and are subject to scrutiny by a judging panel. I was honoured in 2011 to be invited to join that panel, which places strong emphasis on excellence in customer service.

In March 2011, *Betview*'s third annual awards took place at the Grosvenor House Hotel. Twenty five years after Bob Green took the stage at the same hotel to proclaim the importance of customer service, others are following in his footsteps, and I was pleased to have been present for both events.

A competitor to Betview is the monthly magazine *Betting Business Interactive*. This was first published in October 2004 and has to be purchased, unlike *BOS (Bookmakers Office Supplies)* or *Betview*. While Betview focuses on upcoming events broadcast to betting shops and BOS, which launched in 1981, concentrates on the day-to-day matters affecting betting shops and their suppliers, Betting Business Interactive covers the political issues involving the betting and gaming industry. Together with the Racing Post, it means betting shops are well covered in the media and there is no reason for anyone in the industry to be unaware of current topics.

In February 2009 the editor of *Betting Business Interactive* invited IBAS to put forward a monthly piece on its work for publication. I took up the opportunity and my missives have appeared ever since.

At the time I began writing an intriguing episode took place, involving a non-league football match between Weymouth and Rushden & Diamonds. Rumour had it that Weymouth's first-team squad were to strike because of unpaid wages. Insiders at the club and committed fans knew the players' strength of feeling and realised a youth squad, a team of 17-year-olds, would have to take to the pitch against Rushden.

Bookmakers were offering 15-8 for a Rushden win so Weymouth locals, with their inside knowledge, filled their boots and plunged on Rushden, staking an estimated £500,000 in betting shops and £680,000 on Betfair. Punting Weymouth fans had mixed emotions as they watched the game – wanting their team to win – while their money-conscious side was saying 'come on Rushden'. A £100 bet at 15-8 can have a cooling effect on loyalties.

Rushden won 9-0 and none of the betting shop operators refused to pay, taking the loss on the chin. Sometimes the punter knows more than the bookmaker, and with an attitude of 'you win some you lose some', the bets were paid.

With the 2010 World Cup around the corner, football was soon on the agenda again for betting shops. Predictions of a betting bonanza were accurate, and by the end of the competition the betting industry had taken a reported £1billion in turnover.

Despite victory going to Spain, the pre-tournament favourites, most bookmakers reported good profits. This was mainly due to the punter favourites England, Brazil, Argentina and Germany losing in the earlier stages of the competition. Also, because Spain lost to Switzerland in their first game many were deterred from placing large bets on the eventual winners.

An event that produced £1billion in betting turnover would undoubtedly have its disputes and the subject was covered in an article I wrote for *Betting Business Interactive* following the tournament. The article is reproduced below:

The greatest betting event ever, the 2010 World Cup, has finished with the skilful Spanish team becoming worthy winners.

Despite many initiatives on the part of IBAS, and training by betting companies aimed at heightening football betting awareness among front-line staff, the IBAS postbag was heaving during July. In fact, since its inception over 12 years ago, July 2010 was the busiest month ever for IBAS, with football disputes reaching record levels.

Somewhat disappointingly the perennials of wrong prices given, related-contingency multiple bets being accepted in error, confusion between the Golden Boot Award market and top goal scorer market, and the industry standard 90-minute rule, were all to the fore among the disputes.

Just some examples were: bets placed on the day of the final of 'Spain to win' being settled as losers (even though Spain won the World Cup the final was a draw at 90 minutes) unless the bet was clearly for Spain to 'Win the Cup 'or some similar form of words. Bets on David Villa to win the Golden Boot being settled as losers (it was Thomas Muller who won the award, with assists being taken into account) and bets on Muller to be top goal scorer being settled as a four-way dead heat (excluding penalty shoot-outs there were three other players who scored the same number of goals as Muller).

Something that could not have been foreseen was the gods of football conspiring to cause havoc in the betting world through the circumstances of the double of Spain to win the Cup and Villa to be top scorer.

In general 20-1 was a price that could be obtained for a double on Spain to win the World Cup and Villa to be top scorer, on the basis that Spain were 4-1 and Villa was 8-1. Odds compilers, assessing the related-contingency aspect of the proposition (as Villa is a Spanish player) calculated the odds to be around 20-1.

However Villa was in a four-way dead heat for top scorer, hence almost all bookmakers settled bets using their dead-heat rules and divided the stakes by four before putting the divided stake on to the full odds (re Tattersalls rules on betting: Rule 7). The last time that there was a similar occurrence in the World Cup was in 1934!

Thus a £10 double at a price of 20-1 became £2.50 at 20-1, giving a return of £52.50. If odds of 16-1 for the double were taken the £10 double would be £2.50 @ 16-1 giving a return of £42.50. Many customers concluded that this was just another case of the bookmaker acting incorrectly, figuring that if they (the customer) had placed a single £10 bet on just Spain to win (at 4-1) they would have received £50.

At first glance it looks perverse and unfair that a 'successful' double should return the same or less than a single on just one of the selections. A few bookmakers recognised the apparent injustice of settling the bets to their dead-heat rules and offered an enhanced settlement. Others however kept the bet settlements in accordance with their rules.

But despite the apparent injustice, one can see the logic that explains why most bookmakers settled the bets as they did.

Firstly, the double was not wholly successful. One should remember Villa had to share first place with three others. One could say that rather than the bet being successful it was, for the most part, unsuccessful. Customers trying to increase their winnings by combining two bets in a double, risk the possibility of one or both legs of the double being unsuccessful. Therefore, if one of the selections dead-heats, returns are reduced. This reduction is more pronounced if one of the selections has to share first place with three other contenders.

Secondly, would there be as much publicity and would some bookmakers rush to offer overly generous, precedent-setting settlements if a similar scenario repeated itself in the medium of horse racing. Take the example of a £10 double on a 6-4 winner and 1-2 winner, who is involved in a two-way dead-heat. So, £10 at 6-4 returns £25, then £25 on a 1-2 winner that dead heats is settled as £12.50 (half of £25) at 1-2 which returns £18.75 – much less than the single of £10 @ 6-4 which returns £25!

One to ponder?

Politics is always at the fore of the betting industry and it is the main reason why organisations such as the ABB exist, constantly being aware of issues that will affect the industry and being ready to make comments that put the bookmakers' side.

*

Towards the end of 2010 ABB senior executive Tom Kenny summarised five issues that were concentrating the minds of those in the betting industry. The topics have been detailed already but, almost 50 years after betting shops opened, it is interesting to reflect on the topics that are now of particular concern to the industry. The five issues raised by Kenny were:

Unclaimed winnings: The Liberal Democrats, part of the coalition government, and Don Foster MP had again raised the issue of unclaimed monies being used by grassroots sport. Considering customers can claim their money at any time, the industry's position is that if there is doubt as to who any unclaimed money belongs to, the answer is certainly not the local bowls or darts club.

Increase of betting shops in some areas: Some MPs had been complaining at the supposed expanding presence of betting shops in high streets. Labour MP David Lammy was one such politician who seemed to forget it was a Labour government that had dispensed with the 'demand test' and that overall the number of betting shops was decreasing and were estimated to be closing at the rate of four a week.

Gaming machines: The industry was concerned gaming machines were still under probation in the corridors of power, and that they may be subject to further controls. Betting shops are allowed a maximum of four machines and in March 2010 there were 32,934 machines installed in the 8,500 shops. With machines already tightly regulated and accounting for 40% of betting shop revenues, the ABB reminded the government that any deterioration in the terms for category B2 machines would result in shop closures, loss of employment and tax revenue.

Horserace Betting Levy: Since its introduction the levy has caused conflict between the betting industry and horse racing. The conflict has been described as akin to the Hundred Years War. The ABB has called for another funding method to be devised.

Highlighting the economic success story of the betting industry: Betting employs over 40,700 people and pays more in tax than it makes in profit. In addition, the industry excels at operating its business in a socially responsible way. The public should be reminded of this and politicians should be encouraged to laud the professionalism and efficiency of the industry rather than threatening higher taxes and further reviews.

The subject of under-age gambling touches on the involvement that government, via the Gambling Commission, has in the betting industry. But I will leave it to the reader to decide if that involvement is an intrusive and unwarranted one. In 2009 a report from the Commission came as a bolt from the blue to the betting shop industry.

Using mystery shoppers, the Commission had visited sample shops of the major organisations in the industry. These organisations represented 80% of the betting shop industry. The survey found that 98 of the 100 shops visited allowed a 17-year-old to place a bet. It was not suggested that shop employees knowingly accepted bets from an underage person, but the fact remained they did so. It is interesting to remember that a 17-year-old could go to a sweet shop to buy a lottery ticket or scratch card.

*

Senior figures in the Gambling Commission subsequently met with executives of the big five organisations: Betfred, Gala Coral, Ladbrokes, Tote and William Hill. Whatever these discussions entailed, by the time the next survey was carried out later in the year, the position had dramatically changed. In the first survey only 2% of those under age had been refused a bet, but in another later in the year, 65% of 160 shops visited the bet had been refused. I heard on the grapevine that urgent reminders, accompanied by stern warnings, had gone out to betting shop staff, informing them to 'think 21'. Some organisations even introduced a 'think 25' policy.

If staff believed a punter was under 21 or 25, they had to ask for identification and no bets taken until it was proved they were at least 18 years of age.

This policy caused some disruption at betting shop counters because some customers who were questioned about their age became irate that their bets were not taken. Equally, some staff were disciplined for not carrying out the policy. Similar mystery shopper visits were also made to the smaller organisations where 35% of those under age were refused a bet.

Turning back to the nitty-gritty of betting, and the never-ending battle of punter versus bookmaker, the 10 May 2010 will go down as a date to remembered. Some say no one will win as much on horse racing for another 100 years as the Barney Curley coup, which took place on that day. So it was fortunate for the betting shop industry that most of the money was placed on the internet.

The coup involved three of the 11 horses Curley trains and a fourth, Jeu De Roseau, trained by Chris Grant on Teesside. The horses ran at Brighton, Wolverhampton and Towcester and were backed in doubles, trebles and accumulators with various bookmakers. Three of the horses – Agapanthus, Svaranoloa and Jeu De Roseau – won, and were backed down from early prices of 25-1, 8-1 and 7-2. The fourth horse, Sommersturn, finished fifth.

If Sommersturn had won my guess is that many operators would have simply told Curley they could not pay and that he could have their businesses. Not only had Curley got the horses ready to win, but he had also been able to take the early prices the bookmakers had, perhaps foolishly, offered in the morning. So when the horses started to win, bookmakers could not hedge at the odds the bets had been taken at.

Barney Curley.

The coup was subject to an enquiry by the Gambling Commission and British Horseracing Authority but no action was taken against Curley who, at 70 years of age, was still a man to be reckoned with.

*

It is strange the way history has a way of repeating itself. Remember, it was on 24 August 1998 that the *Racing Post* had published incorrect greyhound results. Almost 12 years to the day, on 23 August 2010, a similar situation occurred.

This time, however, it was Turf TV at the centre of the controversy. To the betting shops it broadcast to, Turf TV relayed that the Henry Cecil-trained Wafeira, running at Kempton, had opened at 11-1, shortened to 8-1 then further to 7-1, 6-1, 9-2 and finishing up at 4-1. It appeared to have all the makings of being a steamer in the market and would no doubt have encouraged betting shop punters, as many do, to follow the money and back Wafeira. The horse lost and it was soon learnt that the opening price for Wafeira from the course was not 11-1, as broadcast by Turf TV, but 11-2.

In fact not only was the Turf TV broadcast of 11-1 wrong, so were the subsequent broadcasts of 8-1 and 7-1. Investigations revealed that the correct shows were 11-2, 5-1, 9-2, and 4-1. Broadcasting intentional wrong shows for fraudulent reasons was not suspected but it was believed that after broadcasting by mistake the incorrect price of 11-1, instead of then broadcasting that an error had been made, the subsequent shows of 8-1 and 7-1 were attempts to get to the correct show by stages. Senior executives of Turf TV were appalled at what had occurred, and that the procedures which would have dealt with such a situation had not been followed. Three employees were dismissed for gross misconduct.

Before the end of the year, and the decade, there was one final sad episode in store for the industry. Just before Christmas, IBAS chief executive Chris O'Keeffe had been feeling unwell and was taken to hospital for a check-up. After some checks he was allowed out of hospital to spend Christmas with his family.

Believing Chris was at home I rang him on his mobile phone just after lunchtime on New Year's Eve. He answered and told me he was back in hospital after feeling unwell again. He said he was just sitting around, feeling bored and waiting for another doctor to see him and he asked if I would stay on the line and talk. We had a good chat and, after wishing each other a happy new year, I left him in good spirits.

The next day, 1 January 2011, I received terribly sad news. Chris's close colleague and friend Danny Cracknell, who had been with Chris at IBAS since its inception in 1998, gave me the dreadful news that Chris had passed away the previous evening. He was 56 years old.

There have since been many tributes to Chris. I would like to add my own and say he had a genuine warmth and quick humour about him that was unsurpassed. Chris had a great enthusiasm for the work he did on behalf of the betting and gambling industry, and his contribution

Chris O'Keeffe with some of his administration team at the BOS show in October 2010. Left to right are Sharon Powell, Chris O'Keeffe, Danny Cracknell and me. The other stalwarts of the IBAS admin team, who were holding the fort back at the office, are James Taylor and Bill Baker.

to the industry and its customers was immense and often unsung. He was the life and soul of any gathering, but more importantly he was a true friend. All who knew him miss him greatly.

Following Chris's death I suggested to the board of IBAS that Chris be nominated for a special 'service to the industry' award. The board readily took up this suggestion and made their nomination to *Betview*, who in turn had no hesitation in acknowledging that Chris should be recognised for his work and efforts. His award was given posthumously in March 2011 where over 700 people at the ceremony gave Chris's family – there to receive the honour – a standing ovation.

The start of 2011 and the 50th levy scheme was being negotiated between the bookmakers and the Horserace Betting Levy Board. Once again the parties could not agree. Horse racing wanted the scheme to be one where bookmakers contributed in the region of £140million, a vast increase on any previous year.

Some in the horse racing industry suggested that a strike would be one way to make bookmakers agree to the deal. The bookmakers could not believe the racing industry was prepared to shoot itself in the foot, and at least one bookmaker, Howard Chisholm, confronted the threat saying: 'The quicker they bring about these strikes the better it will benefit everyone. We'll all see it makes absolutely no difference whether racing takes place or not'.

*

Jeremy Hunt, the Culture Secretary who had responsibility for determining the 50th Levy scheme, eventually announced it would be based on 10.75% (previously 10%) of gross profit. The levy would be paid on bets taken on only UK horse racing to raise an estimated £80million. As with all the previous levies there were some caveats to this overview. For this scheme it included the thresholds being reduced from £88,740 to £50,000, thus bringing many more shops into the net for levy payment.

So, where is the betting shop industry now, after 50 years of trading? This is how I would sum it up:

The betting levy is at 10.75% of gross profit on horse racing. Betting tax is at 15% of total gross profit. There are circa 8,500 betting shops, most open seven days a week, 364 days a year (Christmas Day being the exception), and many are open for at least 12 hours a day.

Betting shops have become part of the fabric of British life, contributing £3billion per year to the economy and employing 40,000 staff.

Gaming machines are producing about 40% of betting shop profit and without them at least a third of shops would cease to trade. Betting on horse racing is in decline and football betting is on the up. This is mirrored, and is in part caused, by current day media coverage of sports.

Take Sunday 1 May 2011 as an example. The 2,000 Guineas was run the previous day and was won by Frankel, who produced an incredible performance to rout his Classic rivals in a six-length victory. Another Classic, the 1,000 Guineas is run today. So how do newspapers report these events?

Taking one popular broadsheet and one popular tabloid as examples, the *Sunday Times* has a 16-page sports section in which page after page is given to football, some pages are given to rugby, there are full pages on cricket, athletics and one that gives all other sporting results. And what about horse racing? Just a quarter page, deep inside the paper, covers the Frankel victory, and a further quarter page is used to cram in the cards at Hamilton, Salisbury and Newmarket.

The Mail on Sunday treated horse racing little better in its 24-page sports pull-out. No fewer than 21 pages report on football action, two pages cover cricket, two cover rugby, one is on snooker. One page covers Frankel's victory and shows the racecards of the day. The results from the previous day's cards are squeezed into the bottom of the snooker page.

Punters are still, in the main, writing out bets by hand and, because of this, disputes still arise because of the illegibility and ambiguity of instructions. Marksense slips are used only for football coupons and occasionally for big races such as the Grand National.

Bets are now being paid for by cheque, bankers drafts and bankers card.

*

The EPoS bet-acceptance system has brought many benefits but fraudsters still find ways to con betting shop staff. The 2005 Gambling Act is in force and bets are now subject to contract law and disputes can be heard and a ruling given in court.

There is also IBAS, which continues to go from strength to strength. It has a new managing director in Richard Hayler, fresh from the Greyhound Board of Great Britain (GBGB), where he has left Barry Faulkner, previously of Mecca Bookmakers and the ABB, in charge.

Notwithstanding gaming machines, betting opportunities for punters are almost continuous with greyhound and foreign racing, virtual racing and various forms of numbers betting. In addition there is football, cricket, golf, rugby, tennis and other betting markets. Oh, and there is horse racing.

SIS has a competitor in the form of Turf TV. Betting shop operators are now paying two suppliers and vastly increased fees for roughly the same broadcast service they were receiving previously for just one fee.

Regarding current expenses, an independent betting shop operator will pay £2,400 per annum for a licence for each gaming machine, plus in the region of £5,000 per annum to rent a machine (some suppliers offer machines on a shared-profit basis). There is a payment to the Gambling Commission for a one-shop operator of £1,800 and a fee to the local council for the betting shop licence that varies from council to council, although a fee of £500 per annum per shop is not uncommon. Combined SIS and Turf TV fees will be in the order of £22,750 (this compares to a cost of £14,500 when SIS covered all the racecourses). And the iSIS data feed costs another £4,600. So, before a betting shop operator takes a penny in turnover, he pays out in the region of £40,000 for a two-machine shop per year.

And this is before the normal expenses of rent, rates, light and heat, phone, stationary, equipment, staff and so on have been paid. Once bets are taken there will be the Levy Board waiting to take 10.75% of gross profit on horse bets and the Chancellor of the Exchequer will also be looking for his 15% of total gross profit. If there is anything left, Corporation Tax will need to be paid and the owner will have to pay National Insurance and Income Tax on his salary, and tax on any dividend he may be able to pay himself from the company.

The 'demand test' has gone and a betting shop, with some planning provisos, can open up anywhere. The smaller independents and those with one or two shops are finding trading conditions difficult, partly because of the inequality of levies imposed upon them. It is estimated that betting shops are closing at a rate of four a week

One must also remember that the large multiples have bigger payout limits, a stronger presence and a better-known brand name on the high street than small independents. Thus one can understand why punters choose to bet with the bigger firms.

*

The British Gambling Prevalence Survey 2010, published in February 2011 showed that 73% of the British population gambled, but this included those who played the National Lottery. The figure for those who gambled on other events was 56% of the population, compared to 48% in 2007. So gambling is on the increase – but not necessarily in betting shops.

The growth is mainly coming from the internet. In addition Smartphones enable people on the move to access the internet, peruse the betting market and place bets – all a far cry from 50 years ago.

CHAPTER NINE

THE NEXT 50 YEARS

The joy of writing about the next 50 years is that I will not be around to be told I got it all wrong!

If, as I hope, shows such as the Bookmakers Trade Fair organised by BOS at Wolverhampton, and the Earls Court show held under the auspices of ICE, are still taking place, what services will they be promoting?

Will the idiosyncrasies still remain, such as punters in Scotland calling a bet a 'line', and those in Ireland calling a betting slip receipt a 'docket', will there still be only 12 licensed premises allowed in Guernsey, and will gaming machines still be outlawed in betting shops in the Republic of Ireland? The answer to all those is probably not.

Considering what is happening to the public's sporting interests, betting habits, and reflected media coverage, will the *Racing Post* still have horse racing as its core subject? Indeed, will it still be called the *Racing Post*? 'Blasphemy', I hear some shout.

Given the need to react to what the public want, I would say that the *Post*'s coverage of football will undoubtedly increase and that sports such as golf, rugby and tennis will be given greater coverage. Maybe all of this will be accompanied by a rebranding of the paper's title.

I doubt whether betting shops will continue for much longer to give valued wall space to display only horse and greyhound racecards. Already we see electronic wall displays which can change their content at a touch.

Will some of today's anomalies be causing problems and basic principles be questioned? For instance, what about that great adage, often misunderstood and misquoted by barrack-room lawyers, 'if you can't win you can't lose'. If it ever were true then certainly the

Gambling Act of 2005 appears to have put a big question mark over it.

Section 9 of the Act defines a bet 'to include something that has already occurred, or failed to occur, even though one party to the bet knows the outcome of the event'. So the Act is saying, for example, that two parties can have a bet on who won the 1899 Boat Race. The Act confirms that the bet is ok, even if one of the parties actually knows the answer and the other party only thinks he knows the answer. The bet is legally enforceable even though it can be proved that one of the parties knew the answer.

*

But, how does this work if a punter, maybe a fraudster, manages to place a bet on a selection he knows has won, maybe on an obscure market taking place abroad. Does the legally enforceable bet still stand even though the punter was on a sure winner? Certainly if you bet on some bet exchanges this seems to be the case, as there have been some markets displayed where at least one of the participants, from the options to bet on, had already lost. Nice for the layer, not so good for the backer – a case of buyer beware.

The X Factor-Betfair case mentioned earlier certainly shows that the Gambling Commission are prepared to act decisively when they believe a bet has been struck unfairly. But the interpretation of Section 9 of the Gambling Act does appear to be one that is subjective. An issue I think for the industry is to lobby the lawmakers to have this part of the Act reviewed and clarified.

Maybe the first question for any who wishes to consider what the next 50 years will bring is, will there still be betting shops in 2061?' If it is of any comfort for those newly employed in the industry, not to mention the city financiers who have millions tied up in it, my opinion is a resounding yes. But will they be recognisable to those we have at present? A definite no. And I would say there will almost certainly be fewer than the current 8,500.

But this ignores the fact that newcomers might want to try to muscle in on the custom the betting shop industry has built up by opening quasi betting shops where 'over the counter' sports and racing bets are subservient to gaming machine plays. It seems the Gambling Commission are already concerned at this and are focusing on the interpretation of the meaning of 'primary purpose' in the Gambling Act of 2005.

But for an insight into what may be in store in the near future, go to any greyhound or horse race meeting and you will witness betting, drinking and eating existing happily side-by-side. Betting shops can offer snacks and non-alcoholic drinks but I have no doubt this limited provision will be the next frontier the industry will try to cross.

But in the short term, with the never-ending popularity of gaming machines, surely it will not be long before the maximum of four machines per shop is reviewed and raised. Seeing the queues at some of these machines it is obviously what the public wants. It will raise extra taxes and help to maintain employment.

I would also expect the atmosphere in betting shops will continue to change. The ambience will soften as shops are enlarged and more front windows made transparent. Carpets, air conditioning, public toilets, sofas and high-quality large television screens will continue to be installed. So premises may take on the atmosphere of a coffee bar, rather than a harsh, male dominated, old-style smokey betting shop. Perhaps the 18-35 age group – and women – will stop in.

*

This will go hand in glove with a movement to make betting shops more acceptable. There are some academics who openly proclaim the fact that there are health and social benefits to gambling. One such is Professor Patrick Basham, whose book *A Healthy Bet* extols the social, physiological and psychological benefits to those who bet. This is in addition to the economic benefits through the raising of taxes, that betting brings.

I suspect the number of independent betting shop operators, especially those with four or fewer, will continue to decrease. Over the years many of my colleagues have opened shops in the belief that turnover would come their way as it did when they worked for Coral, Ladbrokes or William Hill. But as many have found to their cost, the name John Smith Bookmakers or Fred Brown Bookmakers above the door does not have the same pulling power as Coral, Ladbrokes or Hills.

One reason is that payout limits applied by the small operator cannot compete with those offered by the national chains. Punters also perceive that the larger operators are prepared to take bets that will be refused by smaller operators.

There is also the ubiquitous high street and internet presence of the major chains. Ladbrokes have cleverly tapped into this brand awareness with the introduction of their loyalty card. So, when away from home, why use the local Joe Bloggs bookmaker when a few yards down the road the red 'magic' sign of Ladbrokes beckons, where one can use the loyalty card.

Possibly the smaller operators' only advantage is at the counter, where a high standard of personal service can be given and good product knowledge and interest in the customers' bets shown.

Betting through Smartphone apps is another serious threat to the viability of smaller shop operators, whereas the larger organisations can embrace such new technologies and increase their business.

Some high street chains also use their shop staff to simultaneously assist in head office functions such as telephone betting. I know of at least one major operator who uses shop staff to take telephone bets. At busy times the calls can easily be re-routed to the shop and, similarly, when the shop gets busy calls can be re-routed back to head office. Economies of scale are wonderful things, and the larger chains have them in abundance.

The scope of betting will also change and in-running or in-play markets and handicap markets will increase in popularity.

There is also the fun of novelty markets which the public and media find amusing. Take the wedding of Prince William and Kate Middleton in April 2011 as an example. Bookmakers were offering odds of 1-5 that the couple's balcony kiss would be on the lips, 4-1 the cheek and 16-1 bar. They were quoting 100-1 that Kate would leave William at the altar, 8-1 that Prince Phillip would fall asleep during the ceremony, 8-11 that the main course at the wedding breakfast would be beef, 6-4 lamb and 100-1 McDonalds or KFC.

*

This part of the industry has been hijacked by Paddy Power, a relative newcomer on the scene. They have turned novelty-bet markets and publicity stunts into art forms. Based in Tallaght, just outside Dublin, publicity is their lifeblood. Paddy Power's stunts include sponsorship of a confessional box in a church and the enormous display during Cheltenham Festival week of the words Paddy Power, Hollywood-style, across Cleeve Hill which forms the backdrop to the racecourse.

For the royal wedding Paddy Power offered bets such as 50-1 Kate (now the Duchess of Cambridge) walking down the aisle in red, 4-1 The Queen wearing a yellow hat and 80-1 about Benidorm being the couple's honeymoon destination. Being the largest betting shop operator in Ireland, the company looked across the water to Britain to satisfy their expansion aims. With the abolition of the demand test in 2007 Paddy Power, from almost a standing start in the first decade of the new century, now has around 125 betting shops in the UK. They were awarded Bookmaker of the Year at the 2011 *Betview* awards.

So, with bookmakers like Paddy Power around, novelty bets will I suspect increase. Will winning coincidences still be thrown up? Of course. But will they be as odd as the horse Royal Wedding winning at Fontwell on 29 April 2011, the same day as Prince William's and Katie Middleton's nuptials? Or Royal Mark winning on 14 November 1973, the day of another royal wedding between Princess Anne and Captain Mark Phillips? Not forgetting Party Politics, who won the Grand National five days before the 1992 General Election.

Regarding in-play football betting, this medium is under the spotlight from FIFA and UEFA. These governing bodies are concerned that in-play markets may encourage the manipulation of games, particularly in markets such as next throw-in, free kick or number of cards issued.

This smacks of shutting the door after the horse has bolted and few British bookmakers have accepted such bets since the episode in 1997 when unusually large bets had been placed on an early throw-in during the match between Manchester United and West Ham – whose Paul Kitson kicked the ball into touch three seconds after the kick off.

Self-service betting terminals in shops may also be the face of the future. Current machines accept only marksense/quickslip-type betting slips on football matches, but perhaps with as many as 200 separate markets in one match. There the machine sits, never going sick or on holiday or reporting for work late, and its cash balances to the penny at the end of the day.

If we are really looking into the future, imagine seeing betting shops with rows of self-serve terminals as in major supermarkets. There are issues of liabilities and bet management, but these are not insurmountable. The payment of bets on self-service terminals can be in cash, similarly to gaming machines and supermarket tills. These, and over-the-counter payments by card will increase, especially with the introduction of cash-loaded cards into the market. No doubt mobile-phone technology will allow users even greater flexibility, so payment via technology built into phones is not unlikely.

*

It will be vitally important for customer-service standards to remain at a high level in the future – they will surely determine success.

Are betting shops up to the customer-service levels of the likes of Marks and Spencer, Sainsbury's, Waitrose and John Lewis? Sadly, with a few exceptions, I don't think so. Go to any of those stores with a genuine problem and it will be immediately remedied – often with some form of compensation.

Compare this to a punter who has been ill-served in a betting shop. All too often a customer will go in with what he thinks is a winning bet, only to be told it has been made void. The punter points out that when he placed the bet he was told he could have it and was given a price. If the customer was unsure what to do, the bet may even have been written out by the shop manager. This then prompts the response that the manager got it wrong, the bet was not acceptable and/or the price was incorrect.

The punter will normally have the firm's rules quoted to him – and often will be the 'obvious error' or 'palpable error' rule, which all operators have, and one they will say allows them to correct any obvious error made by staff.

But the contra argument is that if the error was obvious how did the branch manager make it too? To rub salt into the wound, it is unfortunately almost always the case that the customer is made aware of the voiding of the bet only after it has been 'successful'. This is usually for reasons that, although understandable, are nevertheless frustrating for the customer.

Although some operators are dragging themselves out of the prehistoric era, others have stuck to the philosophy that a war is on, and the bookmaker must give the punter nothing even if they have made a mistake.

Ralph Topping the innovative, forward-thinking chief executive of William Hill, another ex-Mecca man, is leading the charge on raising customer service levels. His 'competition-beating service' initiative, built around staff knowledge of the betting shop product, is a template for others in the industry.

Even though the Gambling Act 2005 turned betting transactions into contracts that were enforceable in law, the industry still waits for its 'palpable error' rule to be tested in a court of record to see if it is upheld.

Customer service levels can be measured, but getting betting disputes right can be a difficult subject. How does one judge if a customer is genuine or is just trying to pull a stroke? There is still the culture among some punters that anything goes and that bookmakers are fair game. It is strange how honest people can suddenly turn like Jekyll and Hyde if they have been undercharged by a cashier. Similarly, when they find they have been overpaid on a winning bet because the settler has miscalculated the return, the punter thinks: 'So what? About time I got something from the bookie'.

*

Some say betting shops are not a normal retail environment where cash is exchanged for goods received. The punter is trying to get the betting shop operator's money, and vice versa. A wise head is therefore needed whenever a customer dispute arises. I would suggest that those operators who survive and prosper will be those who do not act blindly within their rules nor hide behind them.

So when you walk down the high street in May 2036, 75 years after they were legalised, you may not see many betting shops. But those you do see will be large double-fronted establishments, the air conditioning will hit you as you walk in, as will the soft tread of the carpet and the cinema-size screens on the walls. The iced-water fountain and tea bar will also be a welcoming sight.

The screens will be showing sporting events from around the world – cricket from India, baseball from America, football from Brazil. The phrase, heard in the 1990s, that 'betting shops and betting will follow the sun' is here. There will be betting on real and virtual racing – with graphics so good some will find them indistinguishable.

Betting shop owners will have big brand names such as Coke, McDonalds, Gillette and Nike advertising on the racing channels. Racecourses, too, will be advertising their upcoming events.

You'll be able to walk past the rows of gaming machines and order a pizza from the counter – all staff will have to do is take food from the chill cabinet and put it in the microwave, or replenish the automatic betting terminals with till rolls. Walk across to the vending machine, point the iPhone at it and punch in the pin, select the Budweiser option and a bottle of chilled beer is dropped into the serving chute.

You might settle down in the leather sofa, wake up the betting terminal installed in the armrest and put €100 euros on who will score the next goal. Use the iPhone to pay for the bet and collect the printed receipt that whirls out from the terminal.

Ascot may be racing and a few punters could be watching the first race being broadcast on one of the smaller televisions at the back of the shop. But many more will be watching the Spurs v Chelsea game on the big screen. Nice though that Ascot is one of the few racecourses to have survived after the review forced by the parlous state the horse race industry got into when the levy raised by bookmakers declined to a pittance. It was all due to punters forsaking horse racing for other betting opportunities.

As you thank the member of staff for the crisps and nuts just brought to the side table you might ask: 'What time does the shop close today?' The reply, with a smile, will be: 'Haven't you heard sir? New legislation just introduced, we now never close.'

It's May 2061, 100 years after betting shops were legalised and 50 years from now. Walk down the same high street and see how life has changed. People are leaving their offices for a night of entertainment that might include a sporting bar. Government was convinced by the betting and pub lobby that said it was illogical to have separate adult gaming centres, betting shops and bars.

*

The argument went that the licensing of these establishments, and their leisure offering to the public, were similar. People wanted somewhere to go after their daily toil to relax at any hour. Customers can have something to eat and drink in pleasant surroundings while placing bets on the sporting action taking place. They might even pass an hour or so on the virtual betting machines.

Sociologically, it was seen that many wanted places to meet others of a similar ilk. Although the internet and mobile technology had allowed the placing of bets at home and on the move, many would still want to meet and interact with fellow human beings. Bingo clubs, snooker and ten-pin bowling alleys had provided such places in the past. The new sporting bars provide alternative venues for those seeking entertainment, company and social engagement and, yes, a degree of excitement.

It was accepted that casinos offered similar facilities but there was no desire for these new sporting bars to enter the gaming-tables market. Casinos could continue to offer table gaming and machine high stakes jackpot payouts to their members. Sporting bars would be more informal in allowing people instant access with no form filling, and would offer what betting shops and adult gaming centres had previously, but with excellent customer service, high-quality food and full bar services too.

Maybe the innovative CEO at William Hill, Ralph Topping, has already recognised this future. It could be the reason behind his £33.6million purchase of AWI, Cal Neva sportsbook and the Brandywine bookmaking businesses. They are all Nevada-based and operate sports books in casinos and elsewhere. The purchase has been not only of profit but also American sportsbook expertise. With the possibility that there may be a change in legislation covering betting in America, William Hill have put themselves in the driving seat for any expansion.

Back in the UK, the large floor areas of sports bars attract many customers – and they need to with running costs so high. Many that open fail after a few months, much like new restaurants and bars in the 1990s. Some old-style operators cling on from single-fronted shops in secondary shopping areas, offering basic betting facilities, but they struggle. It is rather reminiscent of the 1980s and 1990s when backstreet pubs tried to cling on while the chains like Wetherspoon and Harvester took most of the drinking and casual eating trade.

The larger betting shop chains also have some smaller establishments that do not offer the full sports bar service of their larger sites. But they do provide a welcome facility and service to the local community, with a selection of live sports coverage but with only a limited stock of refreshments and snacks.

It is much like supermarkets whose focus is on airplane hangar sized outlets selling almost anything, but also have smaller express stores for the convenience of the community.

And it will certainly be worth trying to consider what new betting medium might be around the corner. Who would have thought betting terminals would have been the saviour of the industry? Who can guess or imagine what the next iPod of the high-street betting shop might be? Whoever can bring it to market will be both popular and rich, virtually overnight.

*

We shall see, or at least future generations will see.

My tip for any youngster who has just come into the industry: make a note of each month's events. Read and make note of major incidents reported in the *Racing Post, BOS, Betview Betting Business* magazines and any other articles you come across concerning the betting industry. Then, in 50 years time and referring to the contents of this book, you could write a 100-year history of betting shops. What a read that will be.

GLOSSARY

Accumulator Any bet containing more than one selection where the winnings from one part of the bet are carried forward to the other selections. Usually an accumulator is recognised as any bet consisting of four selections or more. A bet with two selections is a double; one with three selections is a treble.

Any-to-come (*see also* Up and Down) Similar to a double or treble, but the customer can declare a sum that should go on the next selection (not in the same race/event) eg £10 win horse A any-to-come £20 to win on horse B. The balance of any stakes and winnings is returned to the customer.

Ante-post A bet in which odds are taken before the day of the event, in the hope that a better price can be obtained. The downside is that if the selection does not take part in the event the stake money is lost.

Banker A selection, in a permutation multiple bet, that must win or the whole bet is lost.

Block method A formula used by settlers to calculate the separate return on doubles, trebles and accumulators.

Canadian Five selections, combined in a full cover of 10 x doubles, 10 x trebles, 5 x fourfolds and a fivefold, a total of 26 bets.

Cold sweat Feeling akin to a panic attack

Combined odds A price given for two (or more) selections to win an event. For example, if one selection is even money to win an event and another is 3-1 to win the same event a bookmaker might offer a combined price of 1-3 for either selection to win.

Crash block method Formula used by settlers to calculate the total return from a full cover multiple bet.

Double An accumulator bet, involving two selections, where any returns from one selection are staked on the second selection.

Double stakes bout A bet involving two selections, and two unit stakes, where the unit stake is put on the first selection and, should there be any returns, up to twice the unit stake is put on the second selection. The process is then reversed, utilising the second unit stake.

Fido A bet involving five selections, covered in 10 doubles and 10 trebles, a total of 20 bets.

Find the Lady A three-card game in which the player has to determine where the Queen is.

First past the post Literally the horse that passes the winning post first. Some bookmakers pay out on the horse that passes the post first, even though it may subsequently be disqualified.

Flag Similar to a four-horse yankee, but with a further 12 bets of single stakes-about bets in pairs, making a total of 23 bets.

Forecast A bet that requires the first and second in an event to be predicted.

Fraction breakdown A bet calculation method used by settlers. The bet returns are found by calculating the bet stake, to the appropriate odds, in a simple step-by-step process.

Frame (in the) A contestant who finishes first, second, third or fourth is said to be in the frame. In some events, such as big golf tournaments, being in the frame can mean contestants who finish further down the finishing order. The term comes from horse racing where the numbers of the placed horses are put into a frame and displayed on a large results board. In police vocabulary being in the frame means one who is suspected of a crime.

Goliath Sometimes referred to as a Genie. Eight selections combined in a full cover of 28 x doubles, 56 x trebles, 70 x fourfolds, 56 x fivefolds, 28 x sixfolds, eight x sevenfolds and one x eightfold, for a total of 247 bets.

Heinz Six selections, combined in a full cover of 15 x doubles, 20 x trebles, 15 x fourfolds, six x fivefolds and one x sixfold, for a total of

57 bets. It gets its name from the number of bets, as in the number of Heinz varieties.

High roller A large-staking customer.

Joint The stand from which a bookmaker at a racecourse operates (the pitch being where a bookmaker puts his joint). The name is derived from the old-style stands that were jointed in the middle so they could be folded in half for easy transportation.

Knockdown ginger A juvenile prank of knocking on a front door and running away.

Knock out A method used by some on-course bookmakers to lengthen the odds of a selection. This is done even though the weight of money bet with the bookmaker does not justify such a price. The reason for the knock out is that the bookmaker has placed a large bet on the selection in betting shops.

Mug A person who is easily deceived.

Pari-mutuel A pool-based system of betting at racecourses in France, the USA and other countries, similar to the Tote in Britain and Ireland.

Patent Three selections, combined in full cover bets, including singles, of three x singles, three x doubles and one treble, for a total of seven bets.

Pitch Place in a racecourse betting ring where a bookmaker stands on his joint to take bets.

Punter Someone who bets or gambles. In any other retail environment a punter would be called a customer.

Rounder Three selections involving three bets. The bets are a single, any-to-come (atc) a double on the other two selections at single stakes (the same stake on the double as the stake on the single). This is repeated for each of the three selections.

Roundabout As a rounder (above) but the stakes are doubled (twice the unit stake) for the double on the other two selections.

Sharks Punters who seek value and bet only when the odds or terms offered are over generous.

Skinner When a bookmaker has taken no bets on the winner.

Sleeper An unclaimed bet with money to pay to the customer.

Swinging Sixties The term used to describe the youth- driven, fashion and culture scene of the 1960s.

Steamer A selection on which the price shortens dramatically following a sudden rush of money that suggests it is well fancied.

Tattersalls Rule 4 A deduction by bookmakers from customer's winnings, through the authority of Tattersalls, to take account of non-runners who were in the betting at the time a bet was placed.

Tissue Odds Provided by a form expert used by on-course bookmakers as a guide for their opening prices.

Tricast A bet requiring the first, second and third to be predicted. With the Tote this bet is a trifecta.

Union Jack Nine selections laid out in such a way to provide for eight trebles. The eight trebles, for selections A through to I are: ABC, DEF, GHI, ADG, BEH, CFI, AEI, GEC.

Up and down (*see* any-to-come) Two selections, two bets. In selections A and B, one stake on A any-to-come (atc) the declared stake to go on to B with any remaining balance returned. Then the process is repeated starting with selection B.